LIVING
Life
IN
ABUNDANCE

PASTOR FREDRICK CHUKWU

First Published 2018, by:
Fame Star Media Ltd.
Unit 17
Studio Court
28 Lawrence Road,
South Tottenham
London
N 15 4ER

+44 (0) 7446234704
+44 (020) 8809 4551
info@famestaragency.com
www.famestaragency.com

Marketed by:
Fame Star Media Ltd.

Unless otherwise indicated, all Scripture quotations in this volume are taking from the Holy Bible, King James Version (KJV), New King James Version (NKJV)

ISBN: 978-0-9957695-3-3

DEDICATION

To my children, Caitlin, Issac and Glory Chukwu. Also, to my late father and mother, Joseph and Marcillina Chukwu.

ACKNOWLEDGEMENT

I give thanks to God Almighty who through His Holy Spirit inspired me into the writing of this book.

I wish to express heartfelt thanks to Fame Star Publishing for her encouragement and partnership on this project from the very beginning. Euphemia Chukwu has given me helpful suggestions that were critical to bringing this manuscript to publication; and without her kindness, understanding and patience, it would been impossible. Thank you, Euphemia.

Also, my Assistant Pastor, Charles Ikekhuah, and Bro. Ephraim Okolo have been quite wonderful helping me to stay focused on the ministry. I appreciate you all.

Special thanks go to my spiritual father, late Reverend Victor Okopi, for laying the foundation of this charismatic renaissance sweeping through the Ministry today. He worked assiduously raising faithful men and women to actualize God's vision for the ministry.

Above all, I remain very grateful to my loving wife, Helen Chukwu, for her keen insight, many hours of assistance and encouragement. She has been my anchor in moments of turbulence in our heavenly race. Thank you my love.

CONTENTS

PREFACE

T his book is designed to lift Christians out of peasantry on to life in abundance in Christ Jesus. From my personal experience, I have realized that the 'Finished Work' of Christ offers humanity a lot more than a usual Christian understands.

When I was 15years old, my father called me one afternoon and said: "My son, I'm afraid enemies may come after your life." He was not what I may call a committed Christian. In his quest to secure my life, he suggested we should meet a member of a secret cult group to initiate me so as to enjoy their protection as well as provision of all that I needed in life. In other words, he was thinking about my living life in abundance with protection through diabolical means as was the practice of many those days.

I declined, not because I was then a fantastic Christian. Though my father would ensure that we all went to church on Sundays even if we were indisposed, he wasn't a believing Christian by any standard. So, to him it was a little Christianity and a little tradition as still being practiced by many today. What was he actually after? Abundant Life!

Not many years ago I gave my life to Jesus Christ and to the glory of God, answered the divine ministerial call. As a pastor seeking the face of God in prayer grounds, camps, and mountains, I discovered the unbiblical practices and confusion among Christians seeking for Abundant Life. The Holy Spirit drew my attention to why He doesn't answer certain prayers offered by many Christians, and why many are not enjoying divine abundance.

In Isaiah 45:19, the Lord says *"I have not spoken in secret, in a dark place of the earth: I said not unto the seed of Jacob, Seek ye me in vain: I the LORD speak righteousness, I declare things that are right."*

During my resting time at a prayer ground, I discovered that 95% of prayer points offered at that ground centred on Satan, the devil, and demons. The rest 5% revolves around God. You only hear the name of Jesus Christ at the end of binding and loosing Satan and demons, and perhaps when they presumably begin to thank God for answered prayers. Then, out they go. That is the end of prayers for that day. Quite sad!

Invariably, they are only magnifying the works of the devil by shouting out only what the devil has killed, stolen and destroyed. Immediately, it occurred to me that there is a missing point here. You may ask: What has Jesus Christ come to do for us? He has said *"I am come that they might have life, and that they might have it more abundantly."* No wonder therefore they never lived in abundance despite their persistent shouting to high heavens.

Each time I encountered this scenario, I would weep in my spirit. It is almost obvious to notice how the devil plays a fast one on many Christians, tricking them into glorifying more of devil's work than those of God the creator of Heaven and earth. Praise God!

This book is carefully structured to assist readers develop deep-rooted consciousness for life in abundance otherwise shrouded in untold mystery beyond human comprehension. It is designed to help Christians embrace the finished work of Jesus Christ for humanity which is all about having life more abundantly. As you read prayerfully, it will help you fulfill life's destiny.

By unraveling the hidden barriers against individual dreams, visions and gifts it empowers and motivates every reader to overcome fear, intimidation, and destructive trap of the enemy (Satan). As you take a tour through this amazing book, you get to learn how to break away from unbiblical traditional and religious norm that has shackled the minds of many Christians. This book will teach you the necessary steps to take in your quest for Abundant Life. I commend you for taking the next step towards becoming a partaker in man's blessedness through the coming of Jesus Christ. In conclusion, my desire is that you are spiritually prepared to claim by faith what Jesus Christ has achieved on earth for us. Stop fretting over what Satan has done or is doing, for it is written, *"Greater is He that is in you than he that is in the world."*

"The thief cometh not, but for to steal, and to kill, and to destroy: I am come that they might have life, and that they might have it more abundantly". John10:10

INTRODUCTION

Living in Abundance has come timely to a generation grappling with so much poverty - in materials and ideas - yet so much wealth all around. Even in the midst of plenty, poverty has descended on many like a consuming epidemic occasioning a rising wave of crime. As you are reading this book, the person next door may be grappling with what to eat or how to afford transport fare to his destination.

Is it the will of God that man whom He has created in His image should languish in poverty on earth and eventually rot in hell on the last day? Pastor Frederick Chukwu's answer is no. In this book, he delves deep down into the scripture to prove that no one should struggle with lack and want. If anything, Chukwu demonstrates that God, from the very beginning, laid a foundation of abundance for mankind to enjoy.

In chapter one, the servant of God draws extensively from the Bible to demonstrate that man, as God's masterpiece, is richly blessed with abundant grace and capacity to determine the course of his life. He concludes that this grace should not be wasted but be deployed to advantage.

In chapter two of this book, Pastor Chukwu uses the imagery of wiring and light to bring out the intricate connection between individual talent and output. He advises everyone to pay attention to God-given talent which he says could only be truncated by sin and disconnection from God, not individual circumstance of birth or the environment.

The human circumstance is subject to the dominion power and will to do exploits which God has abundantly blessed man with. This is the theme of the third chapter in which the author dwells on how to change unsavoury circumstances. The past does not actually determine the future. Therefore man's focus should be on the future, and not the past. Fixation on unsavoury past is rather productive of more failures.

Chapters four and five are the commanding centre of Pastor Chukwu's motivational homily of abundance mentality. In exhorting Christian brethren to develop the mind of Christ, he brings to the fore the power of positive thinking.

The point being made here is that whatsoever a believing Christian conceives in his mind to do, trusting in God as he sets to the task, he shall achieve even much greater than his expectation.

But there are a set of virtuous Christian attitude pertinent to achieving abundance mentality which pave the way to success. One can't do without those set of virtues because one needs them to deal with the challenges ahead which Christ our saviour has invariably overcome on our behalf.

In Chapter 6, you get to know the power of positive confession and how it works. With the mouth, you can either confess your way to abundance or to poverty and sorrow.

But you have to avoid dwelling on the past. The past is good only if it serves as a lesson for the future and not the basis for reaction to the present. For the future, your positive action matters more than your reaction dictated by the past. Put the past behind you and forge ahead, the author counsels in Chapter 7.

In Chapter 8, the tips for developing and maintaining healthy relationships are extensively treated. Good relationships are not only beneficial but also important for actualising your God-given destiny.

However, to maintain healthy relationship, one has to learn to take up responsibility, demonstrate the strength of character to accomplish even tough tasks, and not to give excuses. This is the underlying theme of Chapter 9.

In concluding this inspiring book, Pastor Chukwu says it is inspiring to keep a joyful heart always no matter the challenges that may come your way. God's presence and blessings are attracted only when you are joyful in the Lord just as His spirit abhors an environment of bitterness and acrimony. Therefore, let Jesus Christ be the source of your joy for the joy of the Lord reinvigorates and avails much more than you may imagine.

I invite you to take a tour into this life transforming motivational homily, and experience divine abundance that passes all understanding.

– K. Mgboji

CHAPTER 1

YOU ARE GOD'S MASTERPIECE

"God said, "Let us make man in our image, after our likeness: and let them have dominion over the fish of the sea, and over the birds of the sky, and over the cattle, and over all the earth, and over every creeping thing that creeps on the earth," (Gen1:26).

God's earnest desire for man is to have him live abundant life and live abundantly, too, on earth. In order words, mankind is intended to live joyfully, full of excitement and strength in the Lord, doing great things towards fulfilling his destiny.

Before creating man, God had created lots of what would give him joy and satisfaction. Therefore, mankind was originally intended to enjoy God's superabundance. What a privilege! Consider yourself special and very dear to Him. That is why He had to create other things to service you and He made you in His image.

You must start to see yourself just as God your creator sees you. To God, it's quite disheartening when you fail to live up to the standard He intended for you. God is unhappy seeing His masterpiece (that's you) unable to appropriate His blessings here on earth. He's unhappy to see you helpless, struggling, looking impoverished, thinking that your reward is only in heaven. Oh, no!

Who said your reward is only in heaven? If you believe it, then you are one of those who have failed to take God's written word which says *".....and let them have dominion over....."* Wait a minute! Who is God referring to here? None but YOU. Praise God! I am glad to inform you that you have inbuilt supernatural capability to provoke God's blessings automatically.

Dominion over what? You may ask. *"...over the fish of the sea, and over the fowl of the air, and over the cattle, and over all the earth, and over every creeping thing that creepeth upon the earth."*

FIXED TO OCCUPY

God created you because He knew you are capable of governing the world, and well fitted for the office. He fixed you in it. In creating the earth and all the things

6

therein before creating man, God has demonstrated his tender care and parental solicitude for the comfort and well-being of this masterpiece of His workmanship, which is you. He prepared everything for your subsistence, convenience, and pleasure, before He brought you into being. We may say that the house had been built, furnished, and amply stored for the destined tenant to occupy. But is he ready to occupy?

DESTINED TENANT

Consider this bible passage.
"For whom he did foreknow, he also did predestinate to be conformed to the image of his Son, that he might be the firstborn among many brethren. Moreover whom he did predestinate, them he also called: and whom he called, them he also justified: and whom he justified, them he also glorified," Roman8:29-30.

Of a certainty, man is a tenant on earth while Jesus, the Master, is his Landlord. Man needs to demonstrate readiness for possessing all that the Master has made available for his comfort. It is a question of freewill. God has given man the discretion, freedom of choice. He cannot meddle with man's freewill.

In man's adventure among the Living he is destined to dominate, be glorified and then enthroned. But he has to exercise his freedom of choice as to what he wants. Until then, he can never be partaker of heavenly blessings. He is on earth, not for playing games, but to maintain victory, have good health, enjoy His (God's) protection, provision, silver, gold, bronze, etc. Think about this and take a new position.

GOD HAS GIVEN MAN THE EARTH

It is important to know that you alone can determine what happens to you on earth, not God. It will amount to violation of heavenly order if God intervenes on earth without your invitation or permission.

God Himself has made this categorically clear when He says in Psalm115:16 *"The highest heavens belong to the Lord, but the earth he has given to mankind".*

So, you are God's representative on earth. That is why He consults you first when He wants to ascertain certain things on earth. Not because He does not know. Of course, God is Omniscient, Omnipotent, and Omnipresent but He does not look down on man.

"And the voice of the Lord God came to the man, saying, Where are you?" Genesis 3:9.

Do you now see reasons why you must live in abundance? Actually, it is not what you earn through casting and binding the devil. Neither will you get it by moving from one church to another. It's already inside of you waiting for you to trigger it through acknowledgement of the greater force.

YOU'RE GODS

Psalm 82:6 "I said, You are gods; all of you are the sons of the Most High:"

Think in a minute what our God regards you: *"gods and sons of the Most High."* It literally means that you are His image sanctified and sent on earth to rule. It means that you are a part of God so to speak, capable of calling those things which be not as though they were. It means that you are joint heir with Jesus Christ, partaker of His divine inheritance. It means that you are chosen children of the Most High reproducing good measure of His nature.

Jesus wants us to live with attitude of gods in the world;

9

He wants us to be dependent upon God, deny ourselves and walk humbly.

John G.Lake says "I want you to hear what Jesus said about himself. God was in Christ, wasn't He? An incarnation. God is in you, an incarnation, if you were born again. You are incarnate. So, when Jesus says you are "gods" He is only telling you that you should be aware that:

God is in you, if you are born again.
You should depend upon Him.
You should deny self and follow Him.
You should walk humbly.

Ephesians 4:24 says "And that ye put on the new man, which after God is created in righteousness and true holiness. {true....: or, holiness of truth}
Beloved, God wants you a new man because you are created after Him in RIGHTEOUSNESS and true HOLINESS. He wants you to see yourself the way He has made you. He wants you to take responsibility and authority on earth.

SON-FATHER RELATIONSHIP

2Cor. 6:18 "And will be a Father unto you, and ye shall be my sons and daughters, saith the Lord Almighty.

Just like how you relate with your child, even much better, that is how He relates to you. Jesus has not come for religion because it kills but relationship because it makes alive. Therefore, do not receive the grace of God in vain. Never abuse the privilege or become neglectful of the mercy of God or undervalue the truths in the word of God. God frowns when you are not a doer of what you profess.

Your relationship with Him gets tighter when you fear Him and then He will reveal to you His covenant secret for living Abundant Life.

Psalm 25:14 "The friendship of Jehovah is with them that fear him; And he will show them his covenant."

Beloved, as I am concluding this chapter, you can begin to make progress in your spiritual life now by coming to Christ now. Accept Him in your life as Lord and personal savior. Be bold as a matter of urgency. Always remember, He is your Father and wants to have you. He will accept you no matter your sin. He will purge and sanctify you and dine with you and usher you into Abundant Life.

CHAPTER 2

PAY ATTENTION TO HOW
GOD HAS WIRED YOU

"Even so, let your light shine before men; that they may see your good works, and glorify your Father who is in heaven," Matthew 5:16.

We are here on earth with specific task or role to accomplish. God has given each and every one of us the capacity to attain His plan and purpose. For illustration, let us consider electricity wiring of a house. Each flat has sockets, switches, bulbs etc. It's very important you know what to do when you want to use them; wash and iron your clothes, toast your bread, put on or switch off the lights. I remember the day, when the fuse leading to the light in my room spoilt and therefore could not pass current to my room. I tried and tried till late in the night but could not rectify it though it was a minor fault that didn't take the electrician who understands house wiring a minute to fix. What we are trying to explain here is that you can be frustrated when you don't understand your mission here on earth.

You have been designed or wired with the greatest heavenly material capable enough to change your generation for "the best". What a privilege! You may wonder, what Pastor Fredrick is saying. You are already blessed; a peculiar person, wired to be influenced by a dominion mandate on earth to be attractive to the onlookers!

YOU ARE A GREAT EXPECTATION

"For the earnest expectation of the creature waiteth for the manifestation of the sons of God." Rom 8:19

I have just told you about the electricity wiring in my room which failed to work and how disappointed I was. I tried fixing it, expected and waited for the light to shine but all in vain.

You are a great expectation to the world. You cannot afford to disappoint yourself, the people and your God because He is also watching how you carry-on on earth. A product is meant to meet the consumers' expectation of satisfying their need. You are to show the sustaining power of the gospel in the midst of trials, by the prospect of the future deliverance and inheritance of the sons of God.

The word creature refers to the renewed nature of the Christian with new consciousness that you are made with divine component, desirous of obtaining the full honour and His glory. So you are a sign to other witnesses and not a mockery and that makes you different. As a son of God, your case is therefore different.

GET RECONNECTED

Consider these two bible passages below.
"If you were of the world, the world would love its own. But because you are not of the world, since I chose you out of the world, therefore the world hates you," John15:19.

"Love not the world, neither the things that are in the world. If any man loves the world, the love of the Father is not in him," 1John 2:15.

Malfunctioning is failure to function in a normal or satisfactory manner. When there are defects in our lives as children of God, for sure, we will be disconnected from God and this is the reason for malfunctioning habits you see among Christians of this dispensation.

God says "He chose you out of the world." Think about that in a moment. Why you? It is because you are His peculiar treasure more than all the people. Allelujah! Then He says again, "Love not the world, neither the things that are in the world."

Beloved, get yourself reconnected to His channels of Abundance and it will overflow all over you just like the striking of a match in the midst of darkness.

LET YOUR LIGHT SHINE

"Let your light so shine before men..."

Let your holy life, your pure conversation, and your faithful instruction, be everywhere seen and known, always, in all societies, in all businesses, at home and abroad, in prosperity and adversity, let it be seen that you are real Christian.

God has designed that your presence will be a blessing and a worry at the same time. Yes, many will get worried instead of tapping from the inexhaustible abundance in you because they cannot comprehend the God in you which is the hope of glory.

When your light shines, nobody can kick you aside in taking any decision. No way, it can't happen. They cannot avoid you or do anything of great importance without your involvement. I have noticed that myself! Before I became born again and tapped into the secrets of living Life in Abundance, I wasn't taken any serious within the confines of my environment. But today the story has changed. Almost everybody wants my input in any serious issue. Beloved, when your light is shinning, the world will run after you. Wow! Praise God!

Isaiah 60:1 "Arise, shine; for thy light is come, and the glory of the LORD is risen upon thee. {shine...: or, be enlightened; for thy light cometh}

Understand that you are simply an instrument of divine light placed on the highest mountain and topmost hill diffusing lights to a large number of people.

LIGHT IN THE KNOWLEDGE OF GOD'S WORD

"My people are destroyed for lack of knowledge: because thou hast rejected knowledge, I will also reject thee..." Hosea 4:6.

It is not sufficient to have light. We must walk in the light, and by the light. Our whole conduct should be a perpetual comment on the doctrine we have received, and a constant exemplification of its power and truth.

Work out the promises in your life with fear and trembling. Be fully persuaded that God has started all that concerns you, and will watch over all, till He completes them. Don't seat down and watch the enemy have his way in your life. With fruitless pitying, I see lots of Christian waiting for God to fall from heaven for them even without any spiritual confrontation. It does not work that way always. The kingdom of God suffers violence and the violent take it by force. Don't be deceived! The bible says, *"Whatsoever a man sows, the same shall he reap"* Arise and make a change now in that situation of yours. Walk in the light of the Word of God and you will see yourself navigate into His unspeakable abundance.

Jabez never accepted no for an answer; he then called God of heaven.

"And Jabez called on the God of Israel, saying, Oh that thou wouldest bless me indeed, and enlarge my coast, and that thine hand might be with me, and that thou

wouldest keep me from evil, that it may not grieve me! And God granted him that which he requested," 1 Chron. 4:10.

The bible says: *"And God granted him that which he requested."* Why did God grant Jabez's request but may have not granted yours? Jabez walked in the light of the Word of God and the Light in the word illuminated and eliminated every darkness in his destiny as it cannot comprehend it. Walk in the light of the word and experience the incomparable power of Jesus.

NEVER GET YOKED WITH IDOLATRY

"Ephraim is joined to idols: let him alone," Hosea 4:17.

This is God's summary verdict against Ephraim. God said let him alone, implying that His divine presence has departed from Ephraim.

When you are connected to the idol in any form, you are as well instantly disengaged from abundance heritage. Why are you being deceived into worshipping the image that does not have a functional hand and leg? You will need to carry it along where ever you are going at all times. And at any time you forget putting it in your pocket or in the car, you are in trouble. Think about that!

What a silly labour! Glory be to God that our God is not only mobile but also He is omnipresent (that is present everywhere at the same time). He is also jealous and therefore commanded us thus:

"Do not worship any other god," Exo34:14.

"Do not bow down to them" Exo20:5.

Lest the anger of the LORD thy God be kindled against thee, and destroy thee from off the face of the earth — Deut. 6:15

Flee from idolatry. Our God is completely loving and jealous. Look at the way He dismissed idolatrous Ephraim. "Let Ephraim alone."

Why? Because he is joined to the idol. Imagine the state of a man that does not have the backing of God Almighty? Disaster! Disaster!! Disaster!!!

There is a woman, an organist in a certain church, whose husband opposed her going to church. He was always quarreling with the wife for going to church. He had a little god in his closet which he was serving but the wife did not know. Eventually, a mass retrenchment happened in his place of work. His little god could not secure his means of livelihood. The retrenchment did not only affect him. He was never paid disengagement right many years after. Concerned about the situation of the family, the church prayed fervently with the wife for God's intervention until he was paid N3, 000,000 (about $17,000).

To cut the story short, the wife narrated how she stumbled into her husband's idol one day. According to her, she was searching their house for the new school bag she had bought for their little daughter. As she put her hand inside the wardrobe a little curved instrument fell on the floor. Behold, that is the idol her husband was serving. When the husband returned, he wanted to bring down the roof. He almost beat up his wife. Few months after, the wife stopped going to church.

Today, the situation of the family as at the time of writing this book is better imagined than experienced. The man progressively degenerated till he was finished off by the idol he was worshipping. Guess what? He returned back to his village the same way he had come to Lagos.

The first time I saw the man after his wife stopped going

to church, he told me he was working in a pure water company as a mechanic. He said to me: "Pastor, I will come to see you in your office." But he never came. Another day he saw me passing by and complained that he was going to quit his new job because he was being paid N15, 000 only as monthly salary. Shortly afterwards, I saw him riding commercial motorcycle (popularly called okada) in Nigeria.

When we met a couple of times again his story progressively changed for the worst. He started telling me about his wife and accused her of infidelity. Few weeks after, he approached me and requested to know if the church could give him a space to put up temporarily. According to him, his landlord had parked his load outside meaning they couldn't pay house rent.

The last time he saw me he said he was looking for money to return back to his village leaving the wife and the children behind. IMAGINE! This is the regressive power of the idol.

The bible has made it abundantly clear that *"No man can serve two masters; for either he will hate the one, and love the other; or else he will hold to one, and despise the other. Ye cannot serve God and mammon,"* Matthew 6:24.

21

For goodness sake you are not wired with any instrument of the idol. That is why once you allow idols into your life; it will revote and take dominance, work against the original master plan of God in your life and inflict sorrow and poverty.

Idols do nobody any good. Instead, they are in to kill, to destroy and to steal. Nothing more!

But Jesus Christ, the beloved son of the living God, has come that you might have life and all other things you stand in need of, and have them abundantly, too. Therefore, be serious with God and God alone! You can't serve two masters at the same time. Do not be deceived. Watch clearly to stop anybody from misleading you into worshipping idols.

SHUN UNGODLY COUNSEL

"Blessed is the man that walketh not in the counsel of the wicked, Nor standeth in the way of sinners, Nor sitteth in the seat of scoffers," Psalm1:1.

Let me start by disclosing the sad end of that occult man my father had wanted to introduce me to in his inordinate quest for my wellbeing early in life. Recall how my father, afraid that his enemies might come after my life, suggested I should accompany him to a certain occult man in my village who would have initiated me into their secret society for anticipated protection.

Not many years after my father's failed attempt to get me initiated, the occult man died when it was his turn to donate his blood, leaving behind his wife and children and a filling station which was shut down immediately. But here am I in the Lord bouncing, glorifying His name. If I had taken my father's ungodly advice, definitely you won't be reading this book of mine.

Proverbs 1:10 says "My son, if sinners entice thee, Consent thou not."

Many great people have fallen to wrong counsel. Imagine how I could have also been a victim but God's mercy is sufficient in my life.

Be vigilant over what people tell you because the truth is hidden by the corner of their mouths. They tell you lies to truncate your bright destiny. For many, the devil is just using them to bring the mighty down by their wrong counsel.

Say No:

When they advise you to join their occult.
When they advise you to visit any shrine for money making.
When they advise you to violet the laws of the land.
When they advise you to join evil gang.
When they advise you against your spouse.
When they advise you to embark on illegal and evil ways of making money.

Hear this again, the bible says "Blessed is the man that does not walk in the counsel of the ungodly." So, it is an automatic thing, sort of. Good counsel leads to abundant life. How? The bible says; he shall be like a tree planted by the streams of water, That bringeth forth its fruit in its season, Whose leaf also doth not wither; And whatsoever he doeth shall prosper.

So, I advise you to choose your counselor carefully and prayerfully so that you will not be misled.

Proverbs 15:22 says "Where there is no counsel, purposes are disappointed; But in the multitude of counselors they are established."

My prayer for you dear readers is that, as I am

concluding this chapter the Lord of all creatures will guide your steps to God fearing counselors and also help you discover other secrets to living Life in Abundance as long as you are alive on earth.

CHAPTER 3

CHANGE UNSAVORY CIRCUMSTANCE

"Brethren, I do not count myself to have apprehended; but one thing I do, forgetting those things which are behind and reaching forward to those things which are ahead," Philippians 3:13.

Stop fretting at your circumstance. Create a conducive circumstance you wish to subsist in rather than the unsavory one you've found yourself. For proper understanding, the simple definition of circumstance is a condition that we pass through, modifying or influencing factor of our existence.

I remember many years ago, when we were writing our final degree examination, one lecturer asked me at examination hall what I would like to become as soon as I graduated out of the university? "Bank manger," I replied quickly. Soon, we all graduated. After our youth service, I was in the labour market looking for job but I didn't find any good job about four years after. I must confess that I passed through difficulty situation in Lagos. I would always do a lot of trekking to manage my limited resources.

Now listen. Despite the fact I had not gotten a paid job to justify my BSc, I enrolled with University of Calabar to pursue a second degree. I never allowed my circumstance to hold me down. Then God used my classmate to get me a job and from that time my life changed. Hallelujah! I hope you've learnt something from my personal experience? Never allow your present predicament to dictate your future or stagnate your life perpetually.

I am happy that circumstance changes but our God does not. Well, some body may wish to ask if eventually I became a bank manager as I had wished. No, I never. But I grew to the position of a financial manager in the organization where I worked for six years before I resigned to answer divine call as a full time pastor. Let me tell you, I find joy in what I am doing now much more than ever before. I couldn't have been any more comfortable if I were working as governor of the Central

Bank of Nigeria or any state in the country. Does that sound too good to believe? Believe it or not, there is satisfaction in working in a good place but there is an unspeakable joy and more satisfaction when you have Jesus. Never give up to your circumstances. Stay the course of your good destiny till you get to your desired destination.

EXPECTATION AND DESIRE

"According to my earnest expectation and hope that in nothing I shall be ashamed, but with all boldness, as always, so now also Christ will be magnified in my body, whether by life or by death," Philippians 1:20.

In difficult times, the above bible passage really helps me a lot to stay the course. As I previously narrated, I have always maintained strong expectation of my earnest desires to come through. Hear this: Expectation comes about as a by-product of the alignment of belief and desires.

The account of Isaac in Gen. 26:21 serves as a great lesson to us all. The herdsmen of the land were against him. He had dug a well, and they quarreled and took it away. He dug another one. They confiscated it too. But because he was full of expectation and wanted his desires to come to manifestation, he dug yet another well. This time, his enemies did not quarrel over it. And he named it Rehoboth, saying, *"For now the Lord has made room for us, and we shall be fruitful in the land."*

God has made more than enough room for you to experience abundant life. One thing you cannot hold back is the hands of time. Whether you like it or not time cannot stand still for you. Once it is 2pm, it is 2pm indeed. Anytime you allow your expectation to be cut off you invariably miss out time of your blessing. As the popular saying goes, "expectation is the mother of invention"

PUT THE PAST BEHIND, FOCUS ON THE FUTURE

Apostle Paul told us how to deal with our unsavory circumstance when he said *"....but one thing I do, forgetting those things which are behind and reaching forward to those things which are ahead," Philippians 3:13.*

Let us consider this simple question. If you are searching for something of importance urgently and stumble on some stuffs on your chairs, would you mind them or start arranging them at the same time? No, you can't. The natural tendency is to push those stuffs behind you and continue the search until you find what you are looking for. That is exactly what Apostle Paul is saying. For you to get God's best in your life, you must learn to forget the past. In other words, you must be focused and determined, shunning all distractive influences. It is natural to be tempted to keep looking at your circumstance. Resist the spirit of fixation, and look at your circumstance only with the eyes of "UNSHAKEN FAITH" to change it.

You can't afford to be modern day wife of Lot who, stubbornly looking back against divine instruction turned into a pillar of salt. *"But Lot's wife BEHIND him looked back, and she became a pillar of salt," Gen19:26.*

Lot's wife never wanted to forget the trappings of life in Sodom. She was comfortable with her life in Sodom and preferred that things remained the way they were rather than changing them. Many are like Lot's wife. Never desiring to undertake any adventure to a new horizon, they remain comfortable with the status quo. They are averse to any form of risk because they are afraid of the unknown and lack the will to venture into the terrain of uncertainty. I think that was the case with Lot's wife.

YOU PRODUCE THE MUSIC YOU DANCE

You are like an electro-orchestral type of instrument lumped into divine ability to produce different kinds of sound you dance. You can determine the life span of your circumstance. Stop joking with your life because you can't live in this form forever.

In my church, we once had a member named Ogbonna. He said he was once a member of Osadebe's highlife musical band, a well-known musician in Nigeria. Now, Ogbonna is a Christian supposedly a born again child of God. So, during one of our night vigil programmes, he came out to give a testimony and a special number. The congregation were all happy, expecting to hear an inspiring, modern, professional, and well arranged song. Oh! You will be shocked to hear Ogbonna's special number: it has no meaning, no timing yet he was seriously singing and dancing. He didn't want to stop until the congregation started murmuring.

You can look at your circumstances differently and take another step. Stop producing the kind of Ogbonna sound because it can't take you anywhere even when you're dancing to it. Permit me to inform you that after about a year Ogbonna pattern of singing got better and better. You can also make a change! Take a bold stand and break out from that hold that has kept you from advancing to your God-given height.

Many have done it. You, too, can do even better. Let us consider the account of these four lepers, and pick some wondering leaf from them. Oh, yes. You have to draw some instructive motivation from this bible account.

2Kings 7:3-9 "Now there were four men who were lepers at the entrance to the gate; and they said to one another, "Why do we sit here till we die? If we say, 'Let us enter the city,' the famine is in the city, and we shall die there; and if we sit here, we die also. So now come, let us go over to the camp of the Syrians; if they spare our lives we shall live, and if they kill us we shall but die."

So they arose at twilight to go to the camp of the Syrians; but when they came to the edge of the camp of the Syrians, behold, there was no one there. For the Lord had made the army of the Syrians hear the sound of chariots, and of horses, the sound of a great army, so that they said to one another, "Behold, the King of Israel has hired against us the Kings of the Hittites and the Kings of Egypt to come upon us.

So they fled away in the twilight and forsook their tents, their horses, and their asses, leaving the camp as it was, and fled for their lives.

And when these lepers came to the edge of the camp, they went into a tent, and ate and drank, and they carried off silver and gold and clothing, and went and hid them; then they came back, and entered another tent, and carried off things from it, and went and hid them.

Then they said to one another, "We are not doing right. This day is a day of good news; if we are silent and wait until the morning light, punishment will overtake us; now therefore come, let us go and tell the King's household."

What have you learnt from this Old Testament account? They took their fate in their hands and took a decisive decision. Eventually, they had a breakthrough against debilitating circumstances. But something here is remarkably more important. While they were still leprous, they freely associated with the public so much so they went talking to the King and his household contrary to the Law of Moses. This is the amazing outcome when a determined individual breaks out of the cage.

When you break out of the limiting circumstances, you will be like a gold mill; many will be in search of you! The lepers had gone already into the camp of the Syrians. The bible said "they went into a tent, and ate and drank. The people of Samaria, being led by them into those tents, because there were hungry, they ate and drank with the same plates and cups which the lepers had used. You see, what is still causing that discrimination in your family is that you have not risen up to give a good fight to your circumstances.

YOU'RE GREATER THAN YOUR CIRCUMSTANCE

"Little children, you are of God, and have overcome them; for he who is in you is greater than he who is in the world,"
1John 4:4.

"For whatever is born of God overcomes the world; and this is the victory that overcomes the world, our faith,"
1John 5:4.

Your faith in Jesus Christ empowers you to speak positive things into being, and now is the time you have to exercise that Supreme Force in Christ. Rise up now, cast a look of faith at that debilitating circumstance around you and speak straight to it. Say to it "I'm greater than you, problem." See it as though it never existed. Yes! You are far greater than your circumstance. Stop looking at your size and perhaps your connection.

Cast your mind now shortly at the fight between David and Goliath. Between the two; who is smaller in size? And who is greater in strength? Indeed, Goliath was bigger but he is big for nothing. When I was a child, I used to play a lot with the balloon. Sometimes I would inflate it up as big as a house but at the touch of a sharp little object it would deflate. That is how your circumstance is. Just big for nothing! Though Goliath looked bigger than David, but he was big for nothing. David was full of strength, and actually stronger. That is what I call an "OVERCOMER STRENGTH." David exercised an over-comer strength and overpowered the greatest man of the Philistine.

As the scripture says, *"I can do all things in him who strengthens me," Philippians 4:13.*

What about you?

Are you wondering if you can do it? Yes, you can through Jesus.

CHAPTER 4

ABUNDANCE MENTALITY
– THE MIND OF CHRIST

"For whosoever hath, to him shall be given, and he shall have more abundance: but whosoever hath not, from him shall be taken away even that he hath," Matthew 13:12.

"For unto every one that hath shall be given, and he shall have abundance: but from him that hath not shall be taken away even that which he hath," Matthew 25:19.

T he root cause of lack and want in the lives of many Christians is not that they are not prayerful enough. It is simply because they have got a very wrong mindset. Many Christians have chosen to live in penury all in the quest for heaven. In other words, they build their life on scarcity mandate, preaching that life is all about struggle and self denial. For them any other person who looks better off is a backslider. They end up instilling fear, uncertainty, depression and pressure in the minds of other brethren. But you won't be surprised to see the same self-denying believer grab any gift dangled before him. Instantly, he begins to prophesy positively for you!

If you get nearer to them during their payer time, their prayer changes to this: O' God, my Father, provide for me and my family; Protect bro. Christian and family; his source of bread shall not run dry; and all those kinds of prayers.

But looking down from His exalted throne, God will answer thus: "O' my servant, I have already answered all your prayers but your mindset is your stumbling block; it is dominated by the thought of the devil, not of me. You cannot receive of God what you have not conceived in your mind.

The scripture is final in this case. It says, *"For as he thinketh in his heart, so is he: Eat and drink, saith he to thee; but his heart is not with thee," Proverbs 23:7.*

You are, therefore, the product of your mind. Your mind is the purchasing power of God's abundant blessing. In line with the word of God which says "as he thinketh in his heart, so is he,: Eat and drink...", whatsoever you purchase with your mind on earth big, small or nothing, that is what you will eat and drink. No more, no less.

You are to think optimistically. Develop as much as possible the mind set of making the best or most effective use of what you have. God has created us with a mindset of abundant life. Exercise it, think it and have it.

Stop underestimating yourself unfairly. God has not created you a chicken mind. You are created a great mind to reach out for great things. Take a cue from Adam who was the first man. He had a great mind which was why he was able to cope on earth all alone in the midst of lions, bears, snakes, chimpanzees and giving them instructions before Eve, his wife, was eventually created to be a companion. Beloved, you can never make any reasonable impact on this earth without the mind of Christ.

"Let this mind be in you, which was also in Christ Jesus," Philippians 2:5.

Never labour to promote what Jesus has not come for. He came that we might have life and have it more abundantly. This is the salvation and total welfare He brought to mankind. Remember that He was ever humble, loving, patient, and laborious of which He said his meat and drink was to do the will of his Father, and to finish his work. What are you supposed to do? Have the mind of Christ that you may enjoy this finished work of Christ. A lot of people think they are manufacturing anything new. No! All that you see on planet earth and the one unseen are already in the mind of God. I think it is more appropriate to call it "His finished work". When work is finished I think the next stage is harvest which is the proceeds of the fruitful labour and not to hang in the balance with inferiority mentality.

PUT YOUR MIND TO TEST

"In his days shall the righteous flourish; and abundance of peace so long as the moon endureth," Psalm 72:7.

"O taste and see that the LORD is good: blessed is the man that trusteth in him." Psalm 34:8

When I read the above scripture passages, my life got transformed. First, I began to believe what God has said concerning me. I began to develop my mind for bigger things. Read this story again.

"Before now I was a blind Freddy, lacking the capacity to see and enjoy God's abundance even as I struggled with lack and want. I used to see it as normal life style just as many do, today. But the above scriptures challenged me. I did tell you a little about myself in previous chapters when things were tough and rough after I lost my first job I was managing. Then I refused to fix my mind on the circumstances I was passing through. Instead, I was strong in faith believing God for a new thing. Then we were living in two-bed room flat. I decided to exercise my faith for a big thing. So one evening I went with my wife for a stroll around some undeveloped land around. I pointed to her one upstairs' building and then said to her "that's how our house will stand very soon." My wife laughed and asked "building?" How, how can. She murmured.

Well, I didn't blame her because at that time we were not sure what to eat for that evening and faith does not deny the fact. But I held my peace because my mind had been made up as to what I wanted. I repeated this exercise several times and we walked back home. Oh! Somebody may call it madness. No! It wasn't madness but "Mindset". It is right mentality. To cut the story short, not more than two years after by God's grace I bought a plot of land and built four flats of three-bedroom each of

40

which we are living in one of the flats today.

So, God showers His abundance on the mind that is set. The best way to define abundance in this context is your mindset for your handset. Eh! Fredrick, what are you saying? O, yes. I mean, what has not been set in your mind can never get set in your hand. My miraculous house came because I have already built up the my mansion in my mind for a long time. Then God released it into my hand that was already set to receive.

Do you know what? After every evaporation there is always a down pour. You care to hear this? God is always turning back with the blessing of those whose minds are not stayed in Him. The pregnant person will always deliver only what was conceived. I must tell you now that God is at work in your life now; He is readjusting your mundane mind with His divine mind to fit the blessings about to be released in your life.

REALITIES OF ABUNDANCE MENTALITY

1. "For whosoever hath…"

Matt25:18 "But he that had received one went and digged in the earth, and hid his lord's money."

When the bible says "whatsoever hath", it gives me joy because it simply means that He has given us all what it takes to take over our place here on earth. This is a proverbial mode of speaking. It is simply saying that He has given us a measure of what is more than enough to transform and to take us to our place of rest.

God releases into every one at birth with equal capacity, grace and opportunities. Stop behaving like the Jews who had every opportunity but they would never take a chance. Then the rest of the development of God's gift is left for you. He monitors strictly the application or how we use the gift. Can I put it in another way; God knows all that you are doing with whatsoever you have received from him. Never permit your mind to deceive you that you cannot make it with that little you have now. No, that is wrong mindset. I have seen many end in abject poverty because they never believed God enough in what they are into.

Job 8:7 "Though thy beginning was small, yet thy latter end should greatly increase"

How I wish that man who hid what God has given to him had opportunity to read this verse, perhaps he would trade with that one penny given to him. Unfortunately, he was not faithful with what he hath.

For me I go about laboring in the vine yard of God, which is my ministry work, with all my strength by His grace, waiting patiently for His direction. I know of many who started ministry before me but they fizzled out. Why? They wanted God to bless them with 1000 members overnight. Listen to this truth, when you cannot give account of one member you can't also give account of 1000 members. When you can't appreciate God for the little He has given to you and be ready to be accountable to Him, you are not ready for more of His blessings. I believe, God has given me power to make a change with what is made available to me.

POWER TO MAKE A CHANGE

"According as his divine power hath given unto us all things that pertain unto life and godliness, through the knowledge of him that hath called us to glory and virtue" 2Peter 1:3.

This is the news you have been waiting to hear. God has given you all the power to make a change that will bring about a turning point in your life. Take this home truth. Every genuine change begins from the mind that has been empowered by God. Beloved, you have all the power to bring to yourself all that will give you satisfaction, peace and joy in the Holy Ghost. Yes, get it more clearly that:

1. You have the power to turn that situation around in the name of Jesus.

2. You have the power bring the best marriage out of that shamble home in the name of Jesus.

3. You have the power to resist and cast that devil out of your life in the name of Jesus.

4. You have the power to stay blessed in all areas of your life in the name of Jesus.

YOU GIVE WHAT YOU HAVE

You cannot give what you don't have and you cannot receive what you did not deserve. This is why many are not living in abundance, up to the height that God has designed for them. They refused to walk in the spiritual realm of their mentality to possess their possession. Instead, they walk in physical realm making empty claims of the promises of God.

Any time one tries to give what one doesn't have, I think that one may end up ridiculing oneself. Much of the so called faith exercise is turning out these days as religious gambit. They never have backing power! For instance, somebody who has just lost his job would claim "it's well." Even when he is actually sick, he will say; it's well. If he has an accident, and you ask him, he will reply: it's well.

Yes, empathetically, there is nothing wrong with these answers. After all, the bible says "let the weak say I am strong." But that has to be only when it is coming from your mind backed by strong faith and not just from mere lips. It will end up being a bunch of nonsense and empty claims without any profiting.

Apostle Peter was a man of performance who knows and was sure about what God has deposited in him and on sighting the cripple confronted the spirit thus:

"Then Peter said, silver and gold have I none; but such as I have give I thee: In the name of Jesus Christ of Nazareth rise up and walk," Acts 3:6.

Everything he said on the life of that cripple manifested instantly. The bible recorded that the man walked home healed. You are not only created to live in abundance but also, through you, others will experience abundant life. So, develop the mindset and build on it and you will be surprised to see yourself doing exploits on earth without limitation.

2. "TO HIM SHALL BE GIVEN, AND HE SHALL HAVE MORE ABUNDANCE..."

"Take therefore the talent from him, and give it unto him which hath ten talents," Matthew 25:28.

The higher you develop with enriching your mind with God's abundance, the more He continues to reveal to you the secret to living in abundance. Don't be surprised that you hear me say secret. In life there are secrets to everything just as there are routes to every destination. Abundance of the Lord is shrouded in mystery. The foremost secret is having a sound mentality. Are you not surprised, why some people have waxed great and moved forward, and grew until they became very great? God is committed to blessing people with abundance mentality. Change the way you think and react when you hear about living in abundance and get ready to follow all directions leading to having it.

You ask, Pastor Fredrick, what do you mean? I mean that you just submit yourself to the orders and instructions just like a car owner submits himself to that little device on the car to direct him as he drives to the destination he doesn't know until he gets there. Take up the journey to your abundance today and be careful to listen to your instructor, the little still voice in your mind which is the Holy Spirit.

3. BUT WHOSOEVER HATH NOT, FROM HIM SHALL BE TAKEN AWAY EVEN THAT HE HAS.

"Give not that which is holy unto the dogs, neither cast ye your pearls before swine, lest they trample them under their feet, and turn again and rend you."
Matthew 7:6

God is not a waster. The reason today many are not living in abundance is not that God hates them. No. Or is it that God gives preferential treatment. It is simply because you have failed God. He expected that you will grow but you refused. He has tried to change your orientation but you defied His teachings.

We know that there are many like that today. They are "Mr. I know all" and they are unteachable. Before you quote one scripture they have quoted 30 to counter you. When you look at their life style physically, it all shows in their faces that these ones need spiritual help. I have come across many of them. Do you know what they now do? Moving from one church to another, struggling the pulpit with the senior pastor, causing problems and plotting to swindle the members and to divide the church. Others will resort to more abnormal behaviour like, criticising everything they see and condemning every person that want to correct them. No, you can't satisfy them.

In this case, Jesus cannot do anything for such a fellow. He has no option but to repent and follow the right tract. All that God has given to him, he has misused them contrary to heavenly prescription. In other words, they trampled God's gift under their feet. Then, God will look for another He has proven with His gift and bless him with more because His work on earth will not cease. So, deal with yourself.

ARROGANT IGNORAMUS

"Talk no more so exceeding proudly; let not arrogancy come out of your mouth: for the LORD is a God of knowledge, and by him actions are weighed." 1Sam. 2:3

"The fear of the LORD is to hate evil: pride, and arrogancy, and the evil way, and the froward mouth, do I hate". Proverbs 8:13

There are three sets of people remarkably hinted in the scriptures above. They have a different mindset about abundant life. They believe that they are right and better than everybody. In my life as a pastor I always ask God to help me shield my outward man. You may say eh! Pastor I am not proud; check the following:

1. They are always selfish and get offended when talking about others.

2. They never want to learn but want to dominate and to impose their limited knowledge to others.

3. They get offended when one is appreciated for work well done and ask why not me.

4. They asked questions that are irrelevant to impress others with intention to show off.

5. They oppose every good idea and always want their suggestion given pre-eminence.

The Lord hates the proud and arrogant but the meek and righteous will inherit the earth. What does it mean to inherit the earth? It means to have access to enjoy life in fullness here on earth without limitations. You may be asking what am I supposed to do.

HUMBLE YOURSELF

"Humble yourselves in the sight of the Lord, and he shall lift you up." James 4:10

Jesus is our perfect example. He was humanity and divinity put together yet He made himself of no reputation, and took upon him the form of a servant, and was made in the likeness of men.

You see, Lucifer now satan wouldn't have been suffering in the hands of billions of Christians binding, resisting and rebuking him if he had been humble when he was with God in Heaven. Do you know how many loses satan records each second coupled with everlasting sentence already passed against him, the everlasting condemnation.

"Humble yourselves therefore under the mighty hand of God, that he may exalt you in due time" 1Peter 5:6.

Humility promotes and retains your exaltation to more glorious heights but pride and ignorance demotes, frustrates, and eventually kills. You can't hide your character too long. Why not ask God for the spirit of humility. Many people are scared to do anything tangible with you. Do you think it is because your face is ugly? No! Your character is irritating. You may be too proud and pompous to get on with other people. And this has kept you and your business from advancing. It has stagnated your destiny.

What did you have here on earth that you have gotten by your power? Nothing, all was given to you by God. Then why not use them to serve man and God humbly? When you humble yourself you will enjoy the following: Peace in your family.

Peace with God.
Peace with all men.
Peace in your place of work.
Peace with yourself.
Peace with your visions and dreams.

I earnestly appeal to you from today to keep yourself humble that man and God will find you comfortable dealing with you, using you as instrument of blessings here on earth.

CHAPTER 5

JESUS HAS OVERCOME THE TROUBLES YOU'VE GOT

"I have said all these things to you so that in me you may have peace. In the world you have trouble: but take heart! I have overcome the world." John16:33

God created the world with everything in it very beautiful. All the elemental challenges that arose during creation gave way to the supreme Spirit of God. In fact, God handed to man a perfect earth, an earth without troubles. Therefore man had no cause for binding and casting the devil. Instead, he was enjoying constant fellowship and communion with God. It is not out of place to say that man faced no challenges in the beginning.

"And the earth was without form, and void; and darkness was upon the face of the deep. And the Spirit of God moved upon the face of the waters." Gen. 1:2

So, mankind was created without any troubles on earth until the fall. Troubles of the fallen man are not of God but of the devil. Man having disobeyed God and given up his birthright to Satan on a lease hold, he is now at the mercy of the wicked one who has taken over the earth, causing troubles, pain and sorrow.

"And we know that we are of God, and the whole world lieth in wickedness." 1John 5:19 19

It is very true that wickedness has filled the earth. But in the face of troubles, pain and sorrow, do not indulge in self pity, or seek help from sympathizers who also have their fair share of problems.

The fact of the matter is that you are actually not in any trouble. It is the whole world without Christ that is in real big trouble which is why it is popularly said that "A man without Christ is in crisis." So the present unabated troubles you may be going through are traceable to the following:

Ignorance of the fact that you are still living in the world of trouble.

Ignorance of the fact that it is only in Christ you will find peace.

Ignorance of the fact that you need a lot of patience to overcome the world of troubles.

Ignorance of the fact that Christ has overcome the world, and through Him alone, you too can overcome all troubles.

Ignorance of the Fact That You Are Still Living in the World of Troubles

I am a Nigerian citizen living in Lagos, for instance. I won't claim that I am not living in Nigeria simply because some states in my country are in crisis. No! It doesn't make sense at all. I come across trouble spots sometimes on my way to drop off my children to school, or going on my ministerial work, even sometimes around my church office.

Beloveth, so long as you have life on this planet earth, you will always come across trouble and sometimes encounter it yourself. This may sound unpleasant to many people. They only want to hear peace, in the morning, in the afternoon and at night. But I want to introduce to you peace in the midst of every trouble; morning afternoon and night.

The hard truth is that you cannot live a successful life without experiencing trouble. That is why sometimes you see yourself in trouble that you did not bargain for or cannot explain how it came about. You just wake up from sleep and step on trouble.

Never get worried about that for Jesus said;
"No temptation has taken you except what is common to man. God is faithful, who will not allow you to be tempted above what you are able, but will with the temptation also make the way of escape, that you may be able to endure it." 1Cor. 10:13.

Listen, that trouble you are passing through presently has been weighed by God and He has allowed it in your life because, He as well has given you the strength enough to overcome it. The outcome of every trouble you overcome is blessings. So troubles are allowed on mankind as a training ground for elevation. So your attitude in times of trouble is very important.

"And call upon me in the day of trouble: I will deliver thee, and thou shalt glorify me." Psalm 50:15

Do you know that God is waiting to hear your appropriate response in time of trouble. He is not interested in your murmurings and complaints. Stop going about telling people what you are passing through. Stop screaming for sympathy: Oh! Do you know what I am passing through? I'm suffering! I wear the shoes and I know where they pinch me! Complaints and murmurings add nothing positive to in your life. God says that you should call on Him in the day of trouble. He didn't say you should go about murmuring and complaining.

I always counsel my brethren never to wait to call God in prayers until they are in trouble. Don't wait. Call him every day so that the trouble that you might be into will give you some freedom to speak. For instance, if you are fighting with your enemy and you wait until he holds you to the point that you can't shout again, guess what will happen? Death! But if you start shouting from the onset, then helpers will come.

Nominal Christians today are increasingly waxing cold in prayer. Call them for a prayer meeting, they give you a million and one reasons why they could not make it. Oh! I was busy in the office, put it another time. Oh! I slept off. At other time, they tell you about washing their dirty clothes. Always full of excuses! But when a little trouble knocks on their door, they are the first to come to church, even arrange the chairs. When pastor says in Jesus name, their amen is the loudest. As soon as God answers their prayers, again they disappear into thin air. I call them emergency Christians: they only call on God when it is urgent or convenient.

Stop waiting, only to call on God when you are in trouble. Call Him in trouble and when out of trouble.

IGNORANCE OF THE FACT THAT IT'S ONLY IN CHRIST YOU WILL FIND PEACE

"And let the peace of God rule in your hearts, to the which also ye are called in one body; and be ye thankful." Col. 3:15

Christ is the King and Prince of Peace and it is only in Him any man can find peace. It is He alone that can put off that fire in your life. It is He alone that can save you from the troubled waters of your life. It is He alone that can make that barren womb become fruitful again. It is He alone that can make the dry bones of your life rise again. His name is Jesus! You can shout that name as many times as you like. In as much you abide in Him, and He in you, the name of Jesus will work power and miracle! For it is written, at the name of Jesus Christ, every knee shall bow, of things in heaven and things on earth.

STRENGTHEN YOUR RELATIONSHIP WITH CHRIST, NOT YOUR CHURCH

"The fear of the LORD is the beginning of knowledge: but fools despise wisdom and instruction." Proverbs 1:7

Many Christians are just in church but not in Christ. They have strong relationship with pastor and other influential people in the church but never bother to have a personal relationship with Jesus. I mean, they attend church services, serve in one capacity or the other but they never have any serious relationship with God. The Holy Spirit may have ministered severally to them to get serious but they will bluff the promptings of the spirit. These are mere hypocrites. If you are one of this set of Christians, you are simply inviting trouble in your life because you are living a hypocritical life. You cannot successfully serve two masters at the same time. Beloved, serve God with reverence, and He will sweep away all your troubles and troublers. Then you will see yourself enjoying life in Him.

"For ye have not received the spirit of bondage again to

fear; but ye have received the Spirit of adoption, whereby we cry, Abba, Father!" Rom. 8:15

You are no longer in bondage of fear because you have the Spirit of Jesus which teaches you all things. Why moving from church to church looking for prophets and prophecies?

SEARCHING FOR PROPHET AND PROPHECY

"My people are destroyed for lack of knowledge: because thou hast rejected knowledge, I will also reject thee, that thou shalt be no priest to me: seeing thou hast forgotten the law of thy God, I will also forget thy children." Hosea 4:6

The greatest trouble with many people is lack of adequate information on the word of God. Also, many have chosen the pattern of life they prefer to live. Even as Christians, they would want to live worldly life at the same time. Impossible!

The bible asks: **"Can two work together unless they agree?"**

They have been in a bible teaching church for decades yet they deliberately refuse to comply with the teachings of the ministers.

I have come in contact with many lazy Christians who said their lives were full of troubles. When I started counselling them using the bible they would say "pastor, this is a long process." They would out rightly challenge me to tell them exactly the root cause of their problems.

They would go as far as saying: "O, Pastor! For me to believe you, tell me the colour of the handset in my pocket; the name of my grandfather in the village; the kind and names of tree in my house." When pastor gets them, they scream: O, my spiritual father! You are a very powerful man of God. They want to turn you to fortune teller overnight. If you are one of such pastors, you are already a herbalist in the house of God, multiplying troubles to the troubled. Pastors watch out!

WHATSOEVER A MAN SOWS HE WILL REAP.

"For to be carnally minded is death; but to be spiritually minded is life and peace." Rom. 8:6

Don't you think your carnal nature is taking toll on you? Why are you running up and down, from church to church seventy times seven a year looking for magic? Be spiritually minded and enjoy life in Christ Jesus; you can do all things through Christ that strengthens you.

We are troubled on every side, yet not distressed; we are perplexed, but not in despair; {in despair: or, altogether without help, or, means} Persecuted, but not forsaken; cast down, but not destroyed;

If only you can take things of God seriously as you take your work and worldly things seriously, then you will see God in action destroying the works of Satan and reversing all the evil arrows buffeting you. Stand with the word of God from today and see what difference it is going to make in your life; all the troubles of your life will be swept away.

IGNORANCE OF THE FACT THAT YOU NEED LOTS OF PATIENCE TO OVERCOME TROUBLES

"That ye be not slothful, but followers of them who through faith and patience inherit the promises," Heb. 6:12

Impatience is a joy killer. There is a controlling spirit behind it which does not want any good in our life. Watch an impatient man; he will always miss out God's blessing. I know so many that lost fortunes for lack of patience. Some have got into serious troubles due to impatience.

When I was travelling to my home state for Christmas sometime ago, I learnt a lesson while driving with my entire family on board. I was trying to overtake a big lorry. The lorry driver never wanted to make way for me. But I persisted and succeeded. After I had overtaken the lorry, I sighted through the mirror a boldly written warning: **"BE PATIENT MANY HAVE GONE"**. This warning rang bell in my ears and I slowed down immediately. I didn t want to be counted among the many that had gone as a result of impatience. It was really a lesson for a life time.

"For the vision is yet for an appointed time, but at the end it shall speak, and not lie: though it tarry, wait for it; because it will surely come, it will not tarry." Habakkuk2:3

Your good expectation from God, whatsoever it may be, has a waiting time. Yes, it must surely come to pass but you must wait patiently. Learn to wait on the Lord and stop worrying and nagging in your home. There is appointed time for your expectations to materialize.

Worrying and nagging cannot change anything. Instead, it puts you under pressure with its attendant stress.

When a pastor prays for you, and your expectation doesn't materialize instantly, then the pastor is not truly anointed. You jump to another pastor. For a long time, that has been your habit moving from one prayer house to another. You know all the prayer houses in the city. You will clap hands in one prayer house today and the next day you are in another place of worship, good or bad. Who cares!

I think you need to help yourself. You don't have to continue that way before you get more confused. If you learn to wait, you will surely eat the fruit of the land.

IGNORANCE OF THE FACT THAT CHRIST HAS OVERCOME THE WORLD OF TROUBLE

"These things I have spoken unto you, that in me ye might have peace. In the world ye shall have tribulation: but be of good cheer; I have overcome the world."
John 16:33

Most troubles are a direct outcome of absolute ignorance of the fact that we are overcomers in Christ. We no longer have to struggle to overcome, Christ having given us victory.

Rejoice for the accusers of the brethren have been hijacked and thrown down and are under your foot. When I see some people on the streets with anxiety boldly written all over their faces, I shudder. Their appearance seems like action scenes of a horror movie. You don't have to wear personal challenges and frustrations like a giant's robe upon a dwarfish thief, (I mean oversize garment). Beloved, don't tell volumes about your personal troubles by your appearance or in your conversations.

Rather, be cheerful. You are an overcomer. It is only that you have ignorantly failed to claim your victory. The bible says: "He that is born of God overcomes the world, troubles. Many are real Christ believers but do not have this understanding. They are cheated by Satan. Let me say again, "You are an overcomer". But take note of these: Overcomers don't quit in the face of challenges. And no amount of troubles can weaken their belief in Christ. Even in the worst trying moments, they remain joyful in the Lord knowing that victory is sure.

Daniel in the bible was a perfect illustrative instance. When he noticed a high conspiracy against him and his belief, he did not shudder. He opened his window and prayed three times daily as in normal times. Inside the lion's den, the lion had no power over him as God had sealed the lion's mouth. And he came out unhurt. Learn this from today "your trouble has as no power over you."

IGNORANCE OF YOUR ABILITY TO OVERCOME ALL TROUBLES

"For whatsoever is born of God overcometh the world: and this is the victory that overcometh the world, even our faith." 1 John 5:4

Living the life of an overcomer is living Life in Abundance. To overcome means; to prevail over; to be victorious; to be a master or boss over and to be a conqueror. Beloved, that's who you are here on earth! Is it not exciting? Stop behaving like you have been beaten and helpless. No, you are a warrior with a proof: "you are born of God."

The battle has been won already by Jesus Christ for us all, empowering with a divine mandate to triumph over all troubles of life.

"...For this purpose the Son of God was manifested, that he might destroy the works of the devil." 1 John 1:8

Troubles are the work of the devil and God said He has destroyed the works not the troubles. This means that trouble may keep coming as long as we live on planet earth but the effects of trouble which is always harmful, dangerous, will not overcome us.

So stop praying that God should destroy the devil. No, He will do it but not now. What He has done is to destroy all the works of the devil. Leave the devil alone. If I may ask, have you ever seen the devil? No. But I am sure that you have seen the works of the devil: accidents, sicknesses, untimely deaths, etc. So when God said He has overcome the works of Satan, why bothering yourself calling devil, devil, my trouble, my trouble.

David understood what God has done for us when he affirmed in Psalm 23:4 *"Yea, though I walk through the valley of the shadow of death, I will fear no evil: for thou art with me; thy rod and thy staff they comfort me."*

The trouble with you is that you never perceived yourself as victorious even in the midst of troubles. You have the ability to overcome all troubles which is why the Bible says that you are more than conquerors. When you change your mindset, how you see things around you: I mean when you begin to see those things as nothing before you, as a stranger bound to go back, then you see yourself triumphing over all troubles of life.

"Now thanks be unto God, which always causeth us to triumph in Christ, and maketh manifest the savour of his knowledge by us in every place." 2Cor. 2:14

Believe me, beloved. Your situation is turning around as you put on the breastplate of faith in Christ's victory! You are an overcomer. Cheer up! Rise up from that defeat and move forward unhindered, for you are a triumphant heir in Christ Jesus.

CHAPTER 6

YOUR MOUTH
– AN INSTRUMENT OF LIFE

"A man's belly shall be satisfied with the fruit of his mouth; and with the increase of his lips shall he be filled." Proverbs 18:20

There is power in the tongue: the power to make wealth and the power to destroy; the power to live and the power to kill. In fact, life is shaped by what comes out from the mouth, not what goes in. The words of our mouth frequently shape our good fortune or misfortune in life. This explains the scripture quoted above.

Literally, what remains inside your belly is what enters through your mouth before digestion. In other words you can't eat carrot when your mouth is filled with chocolate. Your belly at beginning can't resist whatever is coming from your mouth. But if it is fruit and crashes with the body metabolism, your belly will be upset. Conversely, it will be nourishment to the body if the consumption is healthy. In the same manner, whatever a man says automatically bears some fruit, positive or negative.

"For by thy words thou shalt be justified, and by thy words thou shalt be condemned." Matt. 12:37

Today, many are not at their God-given best owing to the negative confessions coming out from their mouths. They are continually condemning and cursing, a fact that is working against them. The quickest proof of who a man is, is by what and how he says. By his words, his inner thought and heart is revealed, just as a tree is known by its fruit.

If a man's heart and spirit is right, truthful, pious, teachable, without malice, etc these virtuous attributes will show from the words that come out from his mouth. They will prove that the heart is right. If false, envious, malignant, and impious, they will prove that the heart is wrong, and will therefore be among the causes of condemnation.

I have come across lots of people who heaped failure and

disappointment upon their life even when they are believed to be fire brand born again by reason of their confession. It is rare to hear them speak positive things except when they greet you "Good morning sir." With this obstacle mentality, their fixation is often how this or that thing won't work or be possible. For them, it is only obstacles and impossibilities that they see. This is the reason for so much failure, unripe heart.

UNRIPE HEART

"....for out of the abundance of the heart the mouth speaketh." Matt.12:34

It is never impulsive when you see people talk defeat and failure; they are simply reproducing what is embedded in their heart. The truth of the matter is that you cannot rise beyond your heart's comprehension. You cannot pluck the physical fruit of life that is not ripe in your heart. Break the fallow ground of your heart, keep it fertile for production of God's abundant life.

"Keep thy heart with all diligence; for out of it are the issues of life." Proverbs 4:23 {with...: Heb. above all keeping}

Human mouth is the heart's mouth piece. It communicates to the rest of the body system as well as the world what it sees from the heart. The world and the body system respond to the intent of the heart. The bible enjoined us to *"Keep thy heart with all diligence."* This implies constant and earnest effort to accomplish what is undertaken. It also calls for painstaking effort and hard work in all tasks you set your mind to do. Spiritually, the heart is the seat of the Lord of life and glory; and the streams of spiritual life flows from the heart to all the powers and faculties of the soul. Therefore "put away from thee a froward mouth and perverse lips-and let thy eyes look straight on." In other words, look inward, onward, and upwards.

WORDS NEVER DIE

"But I say unto you, That every idle word that men shall speak, they shall give account thereof in the day of judgment." Matt. 12:36

An old Hebrew saying has it that "Words are living things!" We live in a reality of alterations and manipulations over time. Nevertheless, we are going to give account of every idle word we speak on planet earth, no matter how long or short we live.

Imagine the volume of idle words you may have spoken at age 12, for instance, let alone when you live to be over 100 years. Stop that unprofitable jesting, for it may be working against you. You will be called to give account of it all.

The bible warns us against losing control of our tongues. What you say is a reflection of what you think and what you feel.

That's why, in Matthew 12:34, Jesus says, *"How can you speak good, when you are evil? For out of the abundance of the heart the mouth speaks."*

A number of Bible passages counsel Christians to bridle their tongue as in the following:

The mouth of the righteous brings forth wisdom, but the perverse tongue will be cut off. (Prov. 10:31)

Whoever guards his mouth preserves his life; he who opens wide his lips comes to ruin. (Prov. 13:3)

Whoever desires to love life and see good days, let him keep his tongue from evil and his lips from speaking deceit. (1 Pet. 3:10)

For we all stumble in many ways. If any one does not stumble in what he says, he is a mature man who also is able to control his whole body (James 3:2).

As Christians we should not drop our guard easily in what we say and how we say it to others. Many often regret the utterances they make. We have hurt ourselves and so many others by what we say wrongly. Yes, it is true that we can apologize for what we have said wrongly but we can't withdraw the words that have gone out of our mouth. Take heed, we are judged by the words of our mouth, positive or negative.

WORDS ARE ATTRACTIVE

"There is one who speaks rashly like the piercing of a sword, But the tongue of the wise heals." Proverbs 12:18

It is important we understand how powerful our words are to our lives. They are like a sword drawn, ready to strike at the same time like a healing balm. I remember offending my father a certain day when I was much younger. You had better not been born than enter into our father's trap. That hot afternoon, as he was fuming and getting ready to discipline me, his best friend arrived in our house. He saw me kneeing down and

73

intervened. He begged my father, calling him many fond names. Immediately, the soothing words of his friend healed his wounded heart. And he let me off. That was how the power of words saved me from my father's wrath.

Words have power, beloved.

Many have lost their job, relationship, blessing and promotion as a result of their unguarded utterances. In their place of work, their words and utterances strike like razor sharp jabs at everyone. When you are insulting, harassing, embarrassing, molesting, showing no respect to anyone around you, guess what? People around you will view you with extreme disdain and ridicule. They may mark you out for a target for disgrace, plan to pull you down, or even kill you. But when your word heals, in their heart they will appreciate and stand by you at all times.

YOURS WORDS REFLECT THE FRIENDS YOU KEEP

"One who walks with wise men grows wise, But a companion of fools suffers harm." Proverbs 13:20

Birds of a feather, they say, flock together. You can tell a lot about a person by the company he keeps; they bear the same kind of fruit. The wise move with the wise, the rich with the rich, and the poor with the poor. In the same vein, a cheat, a talkative, slanderer, liar, all are comfortable with their kind.

Know this: everyone is always attracted by one's look alike. A man who is highly educated but the words of his counsel is full of deceit and perverseness will see less privileged people around him always. Important and reasonable people will never take him serious, and will always keep him at arm's length.

LET YOUR WORD BE YOUR BOND

"But let your 'Yes' be 'Yes' and your 'No' be 'no.' Whatever is more than these is of the evil one." Matthew 5: 37

The devil has cheated many believers into telling lairs. Some believers subscribe to this unbiblical tendency to categorize lies into "small lie and big lie". There is what the scripture calls little foxes that spoil the vines (Song of Solomon 2: 15). Every lie or deceit is big before God even if it is as little as an atom.

Unfortunately, this ungodly categorization of lies into "small lie and big lie" is causing a lot of damage in the life of many who subscribe to it. Their attitude to it is "anyhow, let me say this little lies in my work place to get what I want for a living." I once had a boss who was a millionaire but there was no single truth in his mouth. He would lie even against his personal interest. For instance, he would call the account officer for a cheque confirmation. While with us in the Lagos office he would say: "Hello, Mr. Bello! Kindly confirm the following cheques quickly.... because I am in Abuja now." Why telling lies?

In another instance, I was once talking with one of the Evangelists in our church when his phone rang. I overheard the voice from the other end asking him: "Please, are you in the church now? To my surprise, he replied no! Immediately, I picked him up on that, corrected him with love.

Lies are demonic, it's a time bomb, highly destructive and lots of Christians are living in it. That's why it is quite dangerous to have any business dealing with some so called Christian brethren. They will stab you straight in the heart once you drop your guard. Some of them preach excellently the gospel, pray more and better than you, and speak in tongues of fire and thunder. Yet, they take a little chance on you and workout your down fall. It is quite unfortunate how some Christians have lost their salt.

But thanks be to God for the faithful ones who still fear the Lord and speak the truth at all times. Even under duress they stand for the truth. At all times, they refuse to hold the truth in unrighteousness. Yes, they speak up when it matters even against their safety and security.

Let me share with you this story I was told about a commuter bus on transit. I was told that dare devil armed robbers intercepted the bus with 32 passengers on board heading to one of the Northern states. The passengers were asked to deny their fate or be killed. All but 3 of the 32 passenger stood by their faith insisting that Jesus is Lord of Lords and King of Kings. Miraculously, all the 29 people who denied Jesus were killed by the robbers living the faithful three Christians alive.

You can't sustain any relationship with lies. You can do that for only a little time. Sooner than later, observers will discover who you really are and run away from you. Let your yes be your yes and no be your no. Your word should be your bond.

Consider this verse: "Even so, every good tree produces good fruit; but the corrupt tree produces evil fruit. A good tree can't produce evil fruit; neither can a corrupt tree produce good fruit." Matthew 7:17-18

1. Liars are wicked.
2. Liars are deceivers.
3. Liars are greedy people.
4. Liars are against God.
5. Liars are corrupt.
6. Liars are hell candidates.
7. A liar is a dupe.

Beloved, you are candidates of heaven and God's blessing on earth when you speak and stand on the truth always. Stand on the truth even if you are standing alone!

TAKING AN OATH, THE DEVIL'S TRAP

"...but I tell you, don't swear at all: neither by heaven, for it is the throne of God." Matthew 5:34

A certain Christian family once approached me and said they wanted me as a Pastor to preside over an oath to bind them together. They requested me to administer an oath to everyone of them to the effect that none would devise or conspire to devise evil one against another. The family members were afraid, and were pointing accusing finger at one elderly man in one family who was said to have vowed to kill all the members of the other family.

This is a common practice in the world system where the people concerned will go to a shrine and the chief priest will lead them to swear, binding them together against any attempt or conspiracy to harm each other. In fact, when anybody loses anything and suspects some people, they will also go to the shrine to swear. This is the primitive custom of many villages and communities in Africa till today.

So, the family that approached me to administer an oath on them got the disappointment of their lives when I led them to the above scriptures: "… but I tell you, don't swear at all: neither by heaven, for it is the throne of God." They were furious and left for another church where I leant that the priest led them into swearing. It is ungodly for people to swear with bible in their hand, swear in the altar of God. Swearing in the name of Jesus is blasphemy!

This is disobedience!! It is against the law of God!!! Priest, teach your people the fear of God. You don't have to place them in bondage of an oath for them to live in peace with one another. This entirely has negative impact on a destiny. A lot of people have died under oath; some stagnated as a result of the curse they have placed against themselves because of this erroneous practice.

CONFESS POSITIVELY WITH YOUR MOUTH

"Let no corrupt speech proceed out of your mouth, but such as is good for building up as the need may be, that it may give grace to those who hear." Ephesians 4:29

By confessing positively with your mouth, you give God something to confirm in your life. You have to build your life and the lives of others around you by the words that proceed out your mouth. I have to tell you this: If you don't really like what is presently happening in your life, change the words of your mouth! And of course, your heart. Stop blaming the witch and the evil trees in your village for your misfortune or downfall. The devil has expressed enough joy over the negative words coming out from your mouth which he has been using to work against you.

"... but now you also put them all away: anger, wrath, malice, slander, and shameful speaking out of your mouth." Colossians 3:8

Stop speaking in anger! For God is the God of knowledge and He weighs all our heart, mouth and action. You will eventually be what you speak out of yourself. I have leant never to mess my life up by the words of my mouth. Words are powerful and are alive, delivering our confessions to our destinies.

"For with the heart, one believes unto righteousness; and with the mouth confession is made unto salvation." Rom.10:10

Let's together speak what God has commanded us to speak. For me, I never consider my present circumstance before declaring God's best for myself. Some time people around me do think that it is madness. Madness to declare God's word? No! This is wisdom at the highest peak.

I confess prosperity with my mouth every day.
I confess good health with my mouth every day.
I confess God's protection over my children every day.
I confess new open doors with my mouth every day.
I confess God's victories with my mouth every day.

81

Beloved, never be ashamed or tired of confessing of God's
goodness with your mouth, daily.

CLAIM WITH YOUR MOUTH, YOUR HEART'S DESIRE

"For verily I say unto you, That whosoever shall say unto this mountain, Be thou removed, and be thou cast into the sea; and shall not doubt in his heart, but shall believe that those things which he saith shall come to pass; he shall have whatsoever he saith." Mark11:23

Your mouth gives impetus to your blessing. The word that proceeds out of a man's mouth is not a happenstance. It has already been stored in the heart. In fact, the best way to know what the heart is saying is to hear what the mouth says. In the Bible passage above, Jesus is teaching us how the heart and the mouth work interdependently. You notice that the beginning point of a man's failure is when the heart begins to wallow in doubts. Doubt is a thing of the heart and not the mouth. But the mouth is the channel of communication by which the message of the heart is made known. Beloved, if you are not enjoying the fullness of life in Christ, do not blame God.

Do not blame the devil, either. And do not blame your circumstances, too. Go, examine yourself in the mirror. You are likely the problem. You alone can save yourself from yourself. Your surroundings doesn't matter. Why can't you see the opportunities and power Christ has conferred on you thus: "That whosoever shall say unto this mountain, Be thou removed, and be thou cast into the sea; and shall not doubt in his heart... he shall have whatsoever he saith."

Incredible! Whatever mountain still contending with your destiny is the one you have not spoken out of your life as has Christ instructed us to do. My father in the Lord, late Rev. Victor Okopi, told us a story one day about another minister of the gospel. He narrated how Adeyeye who was very thirsty came home one day and drank a liquid he saw in a container in his house believing it was water. The wife, screamed. Adeyeye that is acid! Adeyeye replied: No, it is not acid. That's water! Water!! Water!!! Spoken word is powerful.

The acid turned out to be water indeed. The man is still alive today. The acid was neutralized in his body.

"He that keepeth his mouth keepeth his life: but he that openeth wide his lips shall have destruction."
Proverbs 13:3.

Don't be in agreement with negative beliefs. Let your mindset always be positive. Walk and say things positively by faith, even when the physical realities tend to the contrary. The world is governed by the spiritual realm not the physical. The blessings of earthly existence are obtained by "whatsoever you say" and vice versa.

"He sends his word, and heals them, And delivers them from their graves." Psalm 107:20

Come out from that grave of ignorance! Speak to the mountains of your life, keeping your heart renewed.

RESTRAINED BY A RENEWED HEART

"Don't be conformed to this world, but be ye transformed by the renewing of your mind, that ye may prove what is that good, and acceptable, and perfect, will of God." Rom. 12:2

Your heart will remain raw and unproductive, carnal and worldly if it remains untrained. To us believing Christians, our language is our holy scripture which we read, meditate on and learn daily. This is the most cherished food for the heart after surrendering your life to Jesus Christ. The scripture renews, refines and repositions our heart into changing our view and attitude positively to worldly happenings.

Restrain your mouth from speaking like worldly people who never see nor speak good things around them.

I travelled to my town during Christmas celebration and I happened to meet with my close friend while in secondary school. He was not really looking good. When he came closer, I was put off by the reeking odour of alcohol and cigarette from his mouth. I asked him my bro. what happened? He told me his endless problems: how he tried in the North, South, East, and West but things never worked out. He failed on every side. Now he is doing nothing but looking for money to eat, even that morning.

Oh! I pitied him and gave him some money and invited him to our church the same week. I waited but he did not come. I know his problem, he needed a renewed heart. Really, I wasn't surprised about all the negative things he told me because unrenwed heart is heart full of junks. The mouth will always voice out the contents of the heart. Do not be conformed to the world but be transformed by the renewing of your heart that your mouth will be declaring greatness onto your destiny.

"I have hidden your word in my heart, That I might not sin against you." Psalm 119:11

It is great to tell you that our heart will be filled with the word of God if our life is hidden in Him. Then will our land yield increase, seeking God continuously.

"When thou saidst, Seek ye my face; my heart said unto thee, Thy face, LORD, will I seek." Psalm 27:8

The renewed heart seeking the Lord will have the following characteristics:

1. God's praises: singing spiritual and edifying songs.
2. Constant meditation: Rises early to read and meditate on God's word, avoiding every form of distraction.
3. Reflection on the greatness of God's invitation to know Him.
4. Ask God to make Himself real.
5. Have time for Bible reading.
6. Pray and fast continually.
7. Live a holy life.
8. Evangelize to win lost souls back to Christ.
9. The mouth speaks the mind of God.

Welcome to a new sphere of power where everything is possible by the words of the mouth and the heart is positioned to receive all heavenly heritage.

CHAPTER 7

LIVING IN THE PAST

"And Gideon said unto him, Oh my Lord, if the LORD be with us, why then is all this befallen us? And where be all his miracles which our fathers told us of, saying, did not the LORD bring us up from Egypt? But now the LORD hath forsaken us, and delivered us into the hands of the Midianites.
"And the LORD looked upon him, and said, Go in this thy might, and thou shalt save Israel from the hand of the Midianites: have not I sent thee?" Jugdes 6:13 - 14

L iving life in the past is living backward. It is just like a person looking forward but matching backwards. Great is the fall of a man who walks backward in search of the precious things of the earth. You must know that the world is too competitive that only those who are temperate in all things that obtain an incorruptible crown.

Many Christians are so fixated on the past that they no

longer have the zeal to pursue their deprived God's inheritance. Don't let your past (yesterday) consume your future (today). Stop living in the past. Yesterday was yesterday. It's gone and will never be restored.

So many are living like Gideon who could only see the present circumstance, confined to that situation and never was optimistic about the future.

Beloved, life does not stop at the present irrespective of our current challenge. God has a better plan for us. He is ever with us and cannot forsake us. In trouble or out of trouble He is always working together for our good.

MOMENTS OF LIGHT AFFLICTION

"For our light affliction, which is but for a moment, worketh for us a far more exceeding and eternal weight of glory." 2Cor. 4:17

We are not totally free from affliction. It is very important we understand that whatever situation God has permitted in our lives is a moment's light affliction. Defining this paradoxical expression "Light Affliction" will help us understand more about what I intend to say.

In the context of the word, "Light" means something of low weight and therefore easy to lift; not heavy at all. "Affliction" implies physical or mental distress.

Put together, the meaning of the above paradoxical expression comes clear. It means that a moment of distress cannot be too heavy to overwhelm.

You will believe with me that any affliction that comes to us is not too much to overtake us. That is why the bible says "it is but for a moment" which means that it is short term in nature. God has permitted it and is using it to work out better things for you.

Somebody may wonder if "light affliction" has become God's instrument for blessing man. Before I address this question, let's consider this fact. No nation ever won the world cup trophy without full participation in the contest. In the competition, participants must have experienced physical and mental exertion.

Similarly, in the entire gamut of the scripture, no great exemplary character emerged without passing through a remarkable affliction. Think of Abram, Noah, Moses, Joseph, Job, Elijah, David and many more. The afflictions of the Saviour, Jesus Christ Himself, were legion. But

LIVING LIFE IN ABUNDANCE

they all triumphed!

Understand that there is eternal weight of glory awaiting us. No matter what my today says, I never look at it second time. Instead, I focus on my tomorrow.

Job says: *"Man that is born of a woman is of few days, and full of trouble." Job14:1*

Indeed, life is full of troubles. But thanks be to God who has made it possible for us to emerge triumphant.

YOU'RE A MIGHTY MAN OF VALOUR

"And the angel of the LORD appeared unto him, and said unto him, The LORD is with thee, thou mighty man of valour." Jugdes 6:12

It is quite unfortunate that we do not see ourselves as God sees us. Do we ever realize what God had in mind when He described man as "a mighty man of valour"? Man is God's prepared warrior, His battle axe! We are a change maker, highly positioned and built to cause a delivery of our desired restoration rather than casting aspersions.

God is much ready and available for us, in us, through us

and around us to help us change our ugly past. How disappointing and sad you may look, when your son is beaten up by a much younger person. Many Christians see themselves as incapacitated, always recounting their losses and never want to think a way forward. Let's read what the scripture says about Gideon.

"And Gideon said unto him, Oh my Lord, if the LORD be with us, why then is all this befallen us? And where be all his miracles which our fathers told us of, saying, Did not the LORD bring us up from Egypt? But now the LORD hath forsaken us, and delivered us into the hands of the Midianites." Judges 6:13

This is a testimony of the defeated and downcast who has come to see the present challenge as though it is permanent and without no remedy. So many Christians are of this mindset today asking God Gideon's kind of questions:

Why then has this sickness defied healing? Why then has my spouse run away and refused to come back?

Why then has God not worked out my promotion after putting all my best in the office?

Why then all the disappointments and failures?
Why then God hasn't given me a baby of my choice?
Why then God hasn't killed all my enemies?
Why then am I still in this ugly situation?
Why then God hasn't given me financial breakthrough?

Ignorantly, you have chosen defeat instead of victory as a result of your fixation on the past and present circumstances without sparing a thought for what God is about to do in your life.

The scripture says: *"Remember ye not the former things, neither consider the things of old. Behold, I will do a new thing; now it shall spring forth; shall ye not know it? I will even make a way in the wilderness and rivers in the desert". Isaiah 49:18-19*

We make room for a new thing when we close our eyes on the old things. In other words, if we don't shut a bad door, a new one won't open.

The bible says that old things are passed away. It is important therefore that you consider all your present pains as having gone (the former things and old things) and having no power over you. Do you know what? God is doing new things! Praise God! Even in the wilderness and rivers of your life, He is making a way for you to pass into abundant life.

ALWAYS SEE VICTORY AHEAD, NOT OBSTACLE

No soldier goes to battle having in mind the defeat of the past. No, he will fall by any little attack from the enemy. I have learnt to stay strong in my daily challenge, always looking forward to the victory ahead no matter what is confronting me. God knows that battles are a part of life, so He teaches man on the right disposition knowing that the battle is not ours but His.

For this reason, God says in Deut. 28:1-4:
"When thou goest out to battle against thine enemies, and seest horses, and chariots, and a people more than thou, be not afraid of them: for the LORD thy God is with thee, which brought thee up out of the land of Egypt.
"And it shall be, when ye are come nigh unto the battle, that the priest shall approach and speak unto the people,
"And shall say unto them, Hear, O Israel, ye approach this day unto battle against your enemies: let not your hearts faint, fear not, and do not tremble, neither be ye terrified because of them;
"For the LORD your God is he that goeth with you, to fight for you against your enemies, to save you."

94

We should be glad to know that God is always with us to save us from every battle. Therefore, I shall not be afraid when thousands of enemies shall rise up against me. I don't focus on the present reality of my life. Instead, I focus on the God that overrules and run to Him for refuge.

Recall that as a child, you were fearless challenging older folks in the presence of your parent because in the presence of your parent even a bully dare not touch you. In other words, we had the protection, the insurance cover of our parents. In the same way, we are covered by the Blood of the Lamb; victory is sure.

The Bible says: **"For whatsoever is born of God overcometh the world: and this is the victory that overcometh the world, even our faith." 1John 5:4**

BELIEVE WHAT GOD IS ABOUT TO DO

"And blessed is she that believed: for there shall be a performance of those things which were told her from the Lord." Luke 1:45

The greatest enemy of abundance is "Disbelief." We are professional 'confessors and super prayer warriors' but full of disbelief. God has prepared us like Gideon to be

95

the instrument of deliverance but still we are asking: "…what's this and that." Let's rise up to the standard. Stop moving anti-clockwise by referring regularly to "the former and old things" of yesteryears:

How you had failed yesterday; Where you would have been today if not yesterday's mistake; What you would have gotten today if not yesterday's failure;

How you were defrauded yesterday; How you were denied of your benefits from your spouse yesterday; and all of that.

By so doing, you are only building a pyramid of regrets over your yesterday and at the same time trampling on the blessings of your tomorrow by the words of your mouth. Believe God; believe His word and it shall be established in your life.

The Angel of the Lord told Gideon: *"And the LORD looked upon him, and said, Go in this thy might, and thou shalt save Israel from the hand of the Midianites: have not I sent thee?" Judges 6:14*

God knows all the things you are talking and complaining about. Yet, He is telling us "Go in your might." Whose might? Gideon's? No! In the mighty name of Jesus Christ! You can do all things through Christ who strengthens you. You can turn around your present unpleasant situation in the name of Jesus. God is sending you to do just that and stop talking about yesterday. For your future is brighter than your past!

YOUR ACTION NOT REACTION, MATTERS

"But what think ye? A certain man had two sons; and he came to the first, and said, Son, go work today in my vineyard. "He answered and said, I will not: but afterward he repented, and went." Matthew 21:28-29

Truly, people that live in their past never really want to do or try out anything that might enhance their future. Like a crushed star, they always indulge in self pity. The world is full with God's riches and no one gets any by negative reaction. The world respect, fear and are responsive to action people, not a talkative.

Newton's third law says "For every action, there is an equal and opposite reaction" It simply means that in every interaction, there is a pair of forces acting on the two interacting objects. The bible says again that faith without work is dead. In the midst of that seemingly ugly situation, there is certainly what you can do to work it out Godly way.

I know a sister who would always complain about what her husband had done or failed to do. Each time you hear her speak, she would blame her spouse for her misfortune, failure or missed opportunity. Her reaction and attitude to the past became a stumbling block for expected action of today and tomorrow. That becomes an obstacle to her spiritual and material growth. Life is too short to be spent living in the past.

You may think about the past only to draw up some lessons for the future. Don't allow your unsavoury past determine your attitude to God and draw you away from God's best plans for you. The above scripture says "He answered and said, I will not: but afterward he repented, and went. Here, Jesus commended him, although his reaction was wrong at first (as he attempted to be willful) but he later responded with right action (as he submitted to the will of God). We all may have made this kind of mistake, doing things differently from God's will, but it is proper to make a change of heart if only to step into our destined inheritance. We have to borrow a wandering leaf from Gideon. After his initial negative reaction, he rose to do what God wanted him to do.

CHAPTER 8

DEVELOPING AND MAINTAINING GOOD RELATIONSHIPS

"He that walketh with wise men shall be wise: but a companion of fools shall be destroyed." Proverbs 13:20

Living in abundance is living with and loving one another. We need one another to fulfill our God given goal. You need people in your mission to actualize your vision. Our level of life accomplishment is dependent on our connection strength. God created Adam but realised that two is always better. Then He created Eve as a help meet. Both were connected for better fellowship, communion, companionship and fulfillment.

Living in isolation is living without exploiting all the abundant resources God generously created for man's wellbeing. Your sphere of life will change once you start to relate with godly people. Relationship with the ungodly, more often than not, ends with regrets. Many have been trapped in such relationship, and never had opportunity to share their ugly experience.

The Bible warns thus: *"Be not deceived: evil communications corrupt good manners,"* 1 Cor. 15:33.

We are not all the same until you sincerely confess that Jesus Christ is Lord and son of God. Many have become serial failures because they are into corrupt relationship. One of the things God hates is corruption, the arch enemy of relationship.

"Blessed is the man that walketh not in the counsel of the ungodly, nor standeth in the way of sinners, nor sitteth in the seat of the scornful." Psalm 1:1

Blessed is the man that develops a godly relationship for he will find help in times of need. The bible says, *"He that walketh with wise men shall be wise..."* I can quickly tell who you are once I see your friend. Those you relate with indicate who you really are. The truth of the matter is that when you are into a relationship with someone, you can only give what you have. You can't give what you haven't got.

WALK WITH THE WISE

I have always preached that you only choose wiser people as friends, so that you may learn from them. You can never be better off when you are in the company of people who cannot add value to your life. If you keep company of foolish people, everything about you will over time turn odd and ridiculous.

For me, I am not in a hurry to enter into any relationship. For me, any person I choose as a friend, I have a target of what I stand to gain or impart in that relationship. Don't say but this is selfish. No! It is not selfishness. This is the style of our great Master, Jesus. Every relationship must have intent. Jesus our role model knew that Judas was going to betray Him yet He chose him as one of his disciples

.

Consider this Bible passage. *"And it came to pass in those days, that he went out into a mountain to pray, and continued all night in prayer to God. And when it was day, he called unto him his disciples: and of them he chose twelve, whom also he named apostles."* *Luke 6:12-13*

What do we stand to learn here? First, we should pray

101

before entering into any relationships including choosing our partners, friends and spouse. Many have missed out great opportunities because they are not connected to the right person. God wants us to move with the right people in a right direction because He has great stuff for us all.

BUILDING A STRONG RELATIONSHIP

Like a building, relationship cannot be built in one day. It is built step by step, and over time, it grows strong. No relationship materializes into a strong one overnight. That is where many get it wrong. We are not all-knowing like God, as to know from the outset the other person we want to enter relationship with. Therefore every man needs sometime and prayer to prove a relationship s/he is entering into. It takes time, no matter how little.

The account of David and Jonathan in the bible is a perfect example of what good relationship is all about. It was not built in one day.

"And it came to pass, when he had made an end of speaking unto Saul, that the soul of Jonathan was knit with the soul of David, and Jonathan loved him as his own soul." 1Sam. 18:1

It is worthy of note here that Jonathan's soul was knit to David's. They have proven themselves beyond doubt and any fraudulent abuses. Beloved, don't cheapen yourself from the outset of a new relationship. If you sell yourself quick and cheap, you may live to regret.

First, stay watchful in that prospective relationship, studying the other person to determine if s/he is trust worthy. Many relationships have turned out to cripple and truncate the destinies of many beyond deliverance just as some have helped to actualize destinies of others to the glory of God. Either way it turns out, depends on what you have done or failed to do from the beginning.

RELATIONSHIP DEMANDS COMMITMENT

Commitment cannot be one-way traffic, with one partner issuing all the rules and ensuring compliance at the same time. It has to be a mutual agreement to do something in the future which both partners wish to share together.

The Bible says: *"Can two walk together, except they be agreed?" Amos 3:3*

Most relationships collapse because there was no obligation that restricts freedom of action. This is the reason why many have jumped off matrimonial home, left that office and that relationship even when God has planned to bless them.

Paul's counsel to the Galatians is instructive. *"For, brethren, ye have been called unto liberty; only use not liberty for an occasion to the flesh, but by love serve one another," Gal. 5:13.*

We are to serve one another. In African tradition, the younger are to serve the elder. However, I advise that when you are into a relationship with more established organizations or individuals, irrespective of age, courtesy demands that you honour them. Never expect them to reciprocate with equal commitment. No! They have more engagement than you. They will not come to you as you go to them. You need to keep going until you win their heart. Remember this will take your money, your time, humility and endurance.

RELATIONSHIP DEMANDS FULL DISCLOSURE

"Confess your faults one to another, and pray one for another, that ye may be healed. The effectual fervent

prayer of a righteous man availeth much." James 5:16

Openness is the strong key to a sustainable and lasting relationship. The most difficult and dangerous people to deal with are those with elastic capacity to conceal things, to cover up as long as they wish. They are like time bomb.

I once had a friend who often confided in. I used to tell him my entire secret. But when I noticed that he was always selective about things he disclosed to me, I disengaged myself.

How did I get to know he was selective about things he disclosed to me? Many a time, I would get to know some of things he did from third party. Then I concluded that he was not fully disclosing his faults to me. In other words, there was no full disclosure. He was cagy.

A true and fruitful relationship demands openness to one another. Even God relates to us by the level of our openness with Him.

This is why the Bible warns that *"He that covereth his sins shall not prosper: but whoso confesseth and forsaketh them shall have mercy." Proverbs 28:13.*

In John 15:7, Jesus told His disciples: *"If you remain in me, and my words remain in you, you will ask whatever you desire, and it will be done for you."*

Many people want to assess your degree of honesty before having to do great things with you. Yes, it is not improper. Conduct a self investigation prior to a relationship. That could help you discover things you may not need to pray for again. When you are open-minded, many people will like to do things with you. God will be using many to bless you until you become a blessing.

RELATIONSHIP DEMANDS TRUST

Putting all your trust in man is hard but trusting God is easy and commendable. However, no relationship will survive without some degree of trust. The following are few questions I normally ask and wait for an answer if I must relate with any person:

Can I trust you in my pulpit?
Can I trust you in my church?
Can I trust my members to do business with?
Can I trust you in the area of finance?
Can I trust you with my family?
Can I truth you with my information?

Trust needs levels of test before it is established. So we must be patient about that relationship until we establish trust. In the same way, God cannot give us all we requested at a moment. His method is always a progressive one. He weighs lots of things before granting our request even when we are in relationship because He wants to trust us. So relationship is not an automatic ticket for granting our entire petition. He needs to prove us.

Can God trust you with that child?
Can God trust you with those riches?
Can God trust you with that gift?
Can God trust you in that position?
"He said to her, "What do you want?""

She said to him, "Command that these, my two sons, may sit, one on your right hand, and one on your left hand, in your kingdom."

But Jesus answered, *"You don't know what you are asking. Are you able to drink the cup that I am about to drink, and be baptized with the baptism that I am baptized with?" They said to him, "We are able."* *Matthew 20:21-22.*

From this conversation, we should learn that Jesus can say No to our prayer sometimes because He cannot trust us with our requests when He eventually grants them. When, for instance, we ask for ten thousand members in a space of two years in the ministry, He might be amused in heaven and say we don't really know what we asked.

The question is, can He trust us with a multitude of such magnitude with its implications? He is a progressive God. As we are maturing spiritually, He will add more sheep to the flock. That is God's pattern in other fields of human endeavour.

RELATIONSHIP PROSPERS AS OUR SOUL PROSPERS

I have not seen a couple that never had differences in their relationship but I have seen many that settled their issue without external interventions. I have also seen relationships that got established with mutual benefits within a reasonable time, leaving many wondering what secret behind the success. Speedy consolidation of any relationship is product of a prosperous soul.

"Beloved, I pray that you may prosper in all things and be healthy, even as your soul prospers," says the scripture in 3 John 2.

Prosper' from Latin language "prospero" simply means 'I render happy.' In Greek, the word means something like "to go well with." More especially, the Greek word, eudoo (eudow), means 'to succeed in reaching' or 'to succeed in affairs.'

God's plan is for us to prosper in our relationships. His desire is that things may go well with us, that we will succeed in our affairs. Carnality is the greatest enemy of every relationship. It does not allow truth and transparency to thrive. Instead, lawlessness, fraud and insincerity prevail.

But if we develop our soul to conform to God's law, we begin to think and speak positively, feel good, and respond appropriately. These then will positively affect all facets of our being and create room for abundance in every area of our lives.

RELATIONSHIP EXPRESSES LOVE

"There is no fear in love; but perfect love casts out fear, because fear has punishment. He who fears is not made perfect in love." 1John 4:18

God's relationship with man has being expressed

through His love towards mankind. He relates with us on the basis of love and equality. That was why He took the form of man. Many relationships in this 21st century fall below God's standard. It is characterized by fear, neglect and pride.

In a situation where you cannot freely express your opinion with your spouse, partners, and colleagues it becomes bondage not relationship. Build a relationship that is free of fear, full of lovely expressions and enthusiasm.

Relationship is meant to encourage, build and to mentor one another in the fear of God not to control and make one a servant. This way, you will record more accomplishments in life.

CHAPTER 9

TAKING RESPONSIBILITY

"Now he that planteth and he that watereth are one: and every man shall receive his own reward according to his own labour." 1Cor3:8

God likes active men (doers) and not talkers. We have lots of people who don't walk the talk. They merely talk without acting. In few minutes, they can build castles in the air with their mouth. Many want to live in abundance but never want to take commensurate action towards actualizing their heart desire. Many desire living in abundance daily, confess it daily but never attain to it. Abundant living is achieved when you take responsibility of your divine talent and ability.

Life is frustrating living among people who never take responsibility. They want everything free: free manna, free bread, free fishes, and free cash.

"A sign of wisdom and maturity is when you come to terms with the realization that your decisions cause your rewards and consequence. You are responsible for your life, and your ultimate success depends on the choices you make," says Dennis Waitley, author and coach.

A visit to a newspaper stand in the morning will give you clue of what I am about to say. There, you can hear all manner of untrue stories about what happened inside the state house, White House, and Aso Rock. All are lies, a figment of the imagination. That's what many do daily; they never want to search for gainful employment to change the course of their life.

This, partly, explains the reason for crippling growth in companies and organisations, government ministries, agencies and departments (MDAs) where people do little or nothing to ensure growth and stability. They only wish to eat and benefit from where they never wanted to contribute actively their quota.

LIFE BEGINS WITH RESPONSIBILITY

"And God blessed them, and God said unto them, be fruitful, and multiply, and replenish the earth, and subdue it: and have dominion over the fish of the sea, and

over the fowl of the air, and over every living thing that moveth upon the earth." Gen1:28

Develop passion for working diligently. Whatsoever your hand finds to do, do it with all your heart. Never work only because of the pay but work because of the passion. Be enthusiastic with what you're doing and you will see yourself exceeding your capacity.

Everyone on planet earth was created with the responsibility to get to fulfil one's God-given destiny. You will agree with me that although God provided everything Adam, yet he had a lot to do himself. He has to name all the trees, animals. God created animals and trees without names. So the names of living and non-living things such as cashew trees, fig tree, lion, butterfly, snakes etc were given by Adam. That was his responsibility and he did it very well, which is why today we can't say we don't know the name of this animal or that bird.

Rise up to your responsibility, then you will see that the earth is full of fun and enjoyable.

BE RESPONSIBLE UP-TO-DATE

" .... For unto whomsoever much is given, of him shall be much required: and to whom men have committed much, of him they will ask the more." Luke 12:48

Living life in abundance is not a 'stop over or wait and take' kind of journey. It is for the conscientious, the prepared mind that is readily available to work and accountable for any action or decision.

It is paradoxical that many people want to be promoted but lack the needed diligence. Many wish to be in positions of responsibility: church treasurer, manger, head of department, or head of organization but lack the pertinent leadership quality.

For me, there is nothing wrong with aspirations. But the bottom line is, will you be ready to work and live up to expectation? Stop lobbying to get that position you desire. Instead start living up to commendable level of responsibility and accountability that will endear you to all around you. Living life unaccountable is living life unacceptable.

You get ready to show proof of your calling. Life is all

about evidence. The entire earth and heaven is clear sign of Christ's existence. I do tell people in my church that life is not all about oratory. It is about result. Work hard such that your good work will speak for you. A popular adage says "action speaks louder than voice." Do away with vainglory. Live an exemplary life worthy of emulation by others.

FAITHFULNESS, THE RIGHT KEY

It is impossible to be resulted oriented and become productive on the ground of unfaithfulness.

Faithfulness is the key to maintaining the glow required to match life to the plan and purpose of God. *"Moreover it is required in stewards, that a man be found faithful,"* Paul told the brethren in 1Cor. 4:2.

It takes patience, humility and submission to move to the next level in life. Many folks today are always on the fast lane. Nobody wants to serve any longer. Everybody wants to be a boss overnight. Those whose vaulting ambition is to make it to the top overnight end up cutting corners and doing untoward things. That is why our society is in a mess and avoidable hardship today.

115

Nobody wants to take responsibility!
God demands our Faithfulness.
Man demands our Faithfulness.
Society demands our Faithfulness.
You demand to be faithful to yourself.

1 Samuel 12:24 says: "Only fear the LORD, and serve him in truth with all your heart: for consider how great things he hath done for you."

Prove yourself in your place of work; serve in truth and with all your heart. Then you will see God overwhelming your life with His Abundance. Be faithful all round and God will lift you higher.

TAKE UP TOUGH TASK

Many people want it so cheap and easy but want to gain so much. They tend to forget the popular axiom which says "no work, no pay." Weak people look for weak task and get weak reward but strong people in the Lord go for the 'impossible task to make a mark'. We are not weak but strong enough for any task. We can do all things through Christ Jesus. Let's read the instructive story of this enviable man in the scripture.

Joshua14:12 "Now therefore give me this mountain,

116

whereof the LORD spake in that day; for thou heardest in that day how the Anakims were there, and that the cities were great and fenced: if so be the LORD will be with me, then I shall be able to drive them out, as the LORD said."

The law of living in abundance is just like the law of supply that says: "the higher the price, the higher the supply." Like the economic theory of supply that quantity responds in the same direction as price changes (that is, direct relationship between price and quantity), so also abundance responds to degree of responsibility. The tougher the task, the higher the responsibility, and the more the abundance"

Caleb asked for the mountain! What a great task! He was a record breaker at the age of 85years. If it were many young people of today, they would simply ask for the plain land where they can easily escape when difficulty arises. Life on the mountain is froth with danger. You can be encompassed by the enemy and won't have any escape route. Then you are left with no choice but to confront your enemy, life or death! Yes, Caleb had options but he chose the hard part. He fought and dispossessed the inhabitants and then had Hebron for an inheritance. Look at what the city was like for us to appreciate his effrontery.

Caleb had to fight with the Anakims (very strong and tall people).

Caleb confronted the inhabitants whose cities were great and fenced.

They had trained soldiers with sophisticated instruments of warfare, yet Caleb drove them out forcibly and took over all their belongings.

A soldier is honoured only after a brave accomplishment. Stop under rating yourself, pick up tasks worthwhile and worth appreciating after completion.

"And David longed, and said, Oh that one would give me drink of the water of the well of Bethlehem, which is by the gate! "And the three mighty men brake through the host of the Philistines, and drew water out of the well of Bethlehem, that was by the gate, and took it, and brought it to David: nevertheless he would not drink thereof, but poured it out unto the LORD."
2Sam. 23:15-16

Men of dignity are go-getters. Let your name be written

among the makers- and shakers of the place you have left working. Make a name where you are now! For out the abundance of tough tasks accomplished, the mouth will confess your accomplishments.

EXCUSES, THE GREATEST ENEMY OF RESPONSIBILITY

Abundance mentality has nothing to do with making lots of excuses. Abundance is not achieved on the comfort of your sleeping bed nor will it fall on the lap of the lazy, fearful person. Many will always have a reason for non performance. I have come across lots of people like that. I call them story tellers. You don't make mistake to send them to take a delivery on places where urgency is required. No! They will come back with failure and the attendant reasons.

For those prepared to brave the odds, the outstanding winning mentality of Caleb and Joshua in the story of the twelve spies in Numbers 13:32 is encouraging.

"And they brought up an evil report of the land which they had searched unto the children of Israel, saying, The land, through which we have gone to search it, is a land that eateth up the inhabitants thereof; and all the people

119

that we saw in it are men of a great stature."
Numbers 13:32

Ten out of the twelve spies gave reasons why they might be unable to possess Canaan, the land of abundance. Expectedly, they all perished on the way. But Caleb and Joshua and the children from the age of nineteen years enjoyed their lives abundantly when they successfully took over Canaan.

"Your carcasses shall fall in this wilderness; and all that were numbered of you, according to your whole number, from twenty years old and upward, which have murmured against me," says the Lord in Number 14:29.

We are not helping ourselves when we keep giving reasons and excuses for not:

Being accountable for the responsibility assigned to you.
Getting to your place of work early enough.
Living an exemplary life as leaders.
Being present in church activities.

I know a man who will accept every task assigned to him but never delivers on any. He always has reasons and excuses for non performance. For me, my word for such a person is to 'repent'. God is not author of confusion. He deals with the people according to our dealings with Him. "God says abide in me and I will abide in you"

CHAPTER 10

THE PLACE OF JOY

"Then he said unto them, Go your way, eat the fat, and drink the sweet, and send portions unto them for whom nothing is prepared: for this day is holy unto our Lord: neither be ye sorry; for the joy of the LORD is your strength." Nehemial8:10

Joy is the birth right of every child of God. A place of abundance is a place of joy. Abundance and joy intertwine. They are like inseparable entity that is complementary in nature. Living and staying joyfully is living for all possibility. "Joy is the tap root that sucks God's abundant blessing from the bank of heaven." In order words, it is what makes God's abundance possible in our lives. It is practically impossible to experience God's best without being joyful.

The essence of being joyful implies that your body will acquire the strength and your mind the power and fervor to DO HIS will, and to do it cheerfully, properly tempered with continual dependence on the help of God, blossoming in His presence with meekness of mind, and self-diffidence in deference to God.

This is a powerful means of strengthening the soul. Close the inner mind from seeing and believing on the natural things. By being in such a frame of mind no man will ever fell, and in such a state of mind the general health of the body is much improved. A cheerful heart is not only a continual feast, but also a continual medicine with continual abundance mindset, keeping it as though it is a commandment.

TRUST GOD JOYFULLY

"But let all those that put their trust in thee rejoice: let them ever shout for joy, because thou defendest them: let them also that love thy name be joyful in thee." Psalm 5:11

Every child of God ought to have a conspicuous, continuous, and contagious joy. God bless and defends those that trust in Him joyfully. It is common among Christians to say we trust God for His open door, multiplication and others. But even at that, if you dig deep to ascertain the state of the heart you won't be surprised that the heart is in deep melancholy.

This was the case of the children of Israel on their way out of Egypt. They prayed, murmured and complained. God is not an author of confusion. He is orderly. He did not grant their request because heavenly due process was truncated. They did not pray trusting God joyfully.

Beloved, no matter the trouble, stay joyfully trusting your God. The enemy of living in abundance is the devil who plunges you into waters of affliction. Stay tight with the word of God, your sorrow will be turned into joy!

"Verily, verily, I say unto you, That ye shall weep and lament, but the world shall rejoice: and ye shall be sorrowful, but your sorrow shall be turned into joy." John 16:20

Learn today to stay joyful no matter what you are passing through. Staying joyfully in affliction does not signify that you are rejoicing over what you are passing through but that you are sure that the God you are serving is abundantly able to deliver you.

"If it be so, our God whom we serve is able to deliver us from the burning fiery furnace, and he will deliver us out

of thine hand, O king." Daniel 3:17

I know that you are aware of the end result of this story. They stayed joyfully trusting God and God saved them. This was the case between life and death but Daniel was not quick to undervalue the power of the most High God like many of us will do in this circumstance. Everything is possible in the presence of God when you stay joyful trusting God.

GOD'S PRESENCE IS FULL OF JOY

"Thou wilt shew me the path of life: in thy presence is fullness of joy; at thy right hand there are pleasures for evermore." Psalm 16:11

No one gets into the presence of God with a squeezed face and sorrowful heart. No! It is not allowed in the throne of grace! The guardian angels of God will not allow you in. If you approach a particular office to make an enquiry that is highly important to you, and the first person you see has his face tightened up like a bolt nut, would you go ahead to reckon with him? Wouldn't you go to another person in the same office but with cheerful appearance to make your inquiry? In your mind you will be wondering what's wrong with this person this early morning. God won't accept us either when we are in bitterness of mind. Everyone that comes into the presence of God comes with dancing and rejoicing of heart.

"Rejoice in the Lord always: and again I say, Rejoice."
Philippians 4:4

Rejoicing always is not a function of so much money in your bank account nor your earthly possession but a fulfillment of God's commandment. This real life story will help buttress my assertion.

A certain rich man came back to his village and saw his old school mate on a cashew tree and shouted jokingly in their usual humorous way as in the school days.

"Emma! So, poverty hasn't left you?" The rich man screamed.

"Poor man, have you returned to this village again with your poverty?" Emma replied.

Then the rich man disembarked from his expensive car and said: "Emma, you called me a poor man even as you are here looking for the cashew nuts to eat this morning that you might not die of hunger? Don't you see my car, and my house in this village and other places?

Emma's next response struck a home truth. "Yes, you have money which I lack. But I have one thing which you don't have, and that thing I have is the most important of all.

"What is it?" asked the rich man with curiosity. Emma said, "You don't have JOY!" For some minutes, the rich man couldn't say anything.

You can guess a couple of thoughts racing through his mind at that moment. He said to himself, truly, my friend has made some sense. Wealth and riches that I have, all cannot fetch me the joy I need. But my friend is joyful despite his poverty and
search for cashew nuts to eat this morning.

"Joy supersedes smiling, amusement, happiness, and laughter," said poor Emma. Then the rich man broke his silence, asking his friend what his source of joy was.

THE SOURCE OF JOY

"These things have I spoken unto you, that my joy might

remain in you, and that your joy might be full."
John 15:11

Jesus is the only source of genuine joy. When we find Jesus, accept Him in our lives and abide in Him continually, then, His joy will remain in us. Another word for it is the Joy of the Holy Ghost. This is joy unspeakable, the joy of the friendship and nearness and love of Jesus filling our heart.

The phrase 'abide in Him continually' should be taken seriously because many Christians accept and confess Jesus yet live in misery, sorrow and reproach. As a matter of fact, the most miserable man on earth is not an unsaved man but is a saved man without fellowship with God.

When Jesus abides in you no matter the tears dropping down your cheeks, you will still be joyful in your heart. "Cast me not away from thy presence; and take not thy holy spirit from me.

"Restore unto me the joy of thy salvation; and uphold me with thy free spirit," Psalm 51:11-12.

That was the prayer of penitent David. Even in

penitence, you can be joyful in the Lord just as David.

As I earlier mentioned, the joy of the Lord supersedes all manner of amusement, smiling, happiness that never gets to the root of our heart. Because of lack of understanding many Christians pay money to get joy and at the end of the day they get more miserable than ever.

"These things I have spoken unto you, that in me ye might have peace. In the world ye shall have tribulation: but be of good cheer; I have overcome the world," Jesus Christ counsels his disciples in John 16:33.

This verse specifically say in ME (Jesus) you find peace. You will agree with me that without peace, you cannot be joyful. So if you are looking for joy, stop looking for it from the worldly and natural point of view because Joy is the second fruit of the Spirit, a thing of the spiritual and supernatural.

REJOICE IN TOTAL DEPENDENCE ON JESUS CHRIST

"I am the vine, ye are the branches: He that abideth in me, and I in him, the same bringeth forth much fruit: for without me ye can do nothing." John 15:5

Further scripture passage tells us that it is not by power or by might but by the Spirit says the Lord. Many have chosen to lean on their human understanding and strength. That is why they cannot stand in times of adversity. Depend on God's sovereignty and you will see all things working together for good for you.

When I say that rejoice in total dependence on Jesus, I simply mean that you can get satisfied with any level you found yourself praising God and asking for more. Our God is the owner of everything, who is much willing to satisfy all our needs. You see, when you depend on your human capability, strength and gift, you have rightly told God that you are capable of handling your situation and that is why when you get a slap of disappointment, you feel as if you are carrying the whole world on your head.

"Come unto me, all ye that labour and are heavy laden, and I will give you rest. Take my yoke upon you, and learn of me; for I am meek and lowly in heart: and ye shall find rest unto your souls." Matthew 11:28-29

God is able to give you rest all round.
God is able to grant our heart desire.
God is about to deliver us from the snare of the enemy.

God is able to heal all our sicknesses and diseases.
God is able to give us that victory.

"Now therefore, if ye will obey my voice indeed, and keep my covenant, then ye shall be a peculiar treasure unto me above all people: for all the earth is mine," Exod. 19:5.

God meant well for us! He said if we obey and keep His covenant then we shall be a peculiar treasure unto Him above all people: for all the earth is mine." Depend on Him from today that you may find new Joy that supersedes every event.

"For his anger endureth but a moment; in his favour is life: weeping may endure for a night, but joy cometh in the morning," Psalm 30:5.

For certain, when we depend on him joyfully, no matter our night of troubles, He will turn things around before morning. Stop believing that things will remain the same. No! Our God is God of change. He remains the same but changes all things, even our circumstances. Many have gone to bed with afflictions, depression, distraction, heaviness of the heart, but woke up sound, hearty, and healed singing songs of Joy.

JOY STIRS UP SPIRITUAL SONGS

This is not the kind of song you sing when you receive unexpected gift. Neither is it the kind of song you find the hymn books nor the one you read on the screen during your church services. These are songs sent by the Holy Ghost into our inner heart filled with joy and excitement and quickened in our mouth either in known or unknown language.

This spiritual experience is captured in Ephesians 5:19 thus: *"Speaking to yourselves in psalms and hymns and spiritual songs, singing and making melody in your heart to the Lord."*

Believe me this is the type of song that shakes the heaven and gladden the heart of God of heaven and earth.

I remember vividly one day as I was about taking my bath, I burst out singing songs in an unknown language and I remained in the bathroom far more than expected without pouring water on myself before it dawned on me that I was actually in the bathroom for shower. I was consumed in His presence right inside my bathroom. This is spiritual song. God quickens it in your heart, and lifts it out of your mouth and you will not be bothered how it sounds no matter where you are. You will sing the song it freely. This is clear evidence that your spirit man is alive and joyous. At this point everything is possible!

This is unique expression of belonging.
This is an expression of thankfulness and joyfulness.
It is a demonstration of cheerfulness and trustworthiness.
It is an evidence of spiritual fruitfulness and inner tranquility.
This is enthroning His faithfulness and exaltation.

This is a demonstration of belief in the blessedness of adorable, inconceivably beautiful Son of God, Jesus. It is a delightful experience you would like to happen over and over again because it automatically takes your mind from the mundane surroundings to the supernatural realm with an overwhelming spiritual relevance:

It builds up the spirit.
It maintains purity of heart and life.
It is remedy against sin.
It grants you confidence in times of trouble.
It launches you into deep prayers to God.
It gives satisfaction on loving kindness of God.

It makes us to love and to submit to one another in the fear of God.

It brings to an end to any sorrowful feeling.

It unveils the heavenly secret.

It promotes the glory of God.

Living life in abundance is life full of Joy in the Holy Ghost.

Stay joyful even in the time of trouble then will you live to testify that the storm is actually over.

"All the days of the afflicted are evil: but he that is of a merry heart hath a continual feast." Proverbs 15:15

This is living in satisfaction, overflow, praises, songs of thanksgiving, giving glory to God. Beloved, abundant life is for you and for me. This is what God ordained from the foundation of the earth for us. Rise up to it; it is our inheritance in Christ Jesus.

CONCLUSION:

The Spirit of God is changing us all the time. All the circumstances of our lives are included in the process of a transformation into living abundant life. He wants us to be like His Son, in full confidence that we can do all things through Him strengthening us. Our part is to be willing to step out of the old belief system and habit into newness of life to enjoy all the works of Christ in the cross.

Abundant living is not for a selected few but for all of us, the joint heirs with Christ.

About the Author

FREDRICK O.CHUKWU is a dynamic teacher of the word, an Evangelist, international motivational speaker, a marriage and Relationship Counselor, business consultant, author of The Vanity of Prayers and The Lost Focus. His London-based radio program has been a blessing to millions of people across the globe.

Pastor Chukwu is the founder of Abundant Touch Ministries World Wide, the spiritual director of Abundant Camp Prayer Mountain situated in Enugu State. He is the senior pastor of Faith Abundant Ministry International located in Ejigbo, Lagos State, Nigeria.

He holds a Bachelor of Science degree (BSc.) in Banking and a Masters degree in Business Administration (MBA). He is married with three children to the glory of God.

We hope you enjoyed reading this book, Living Life in Abundance?

For more information and other publications from the same author, visit our website at:

www.faithabundantministryintl.org.

You can also contact:

FAITH ABUNDANT MINISTRY INTERNATIONAL
17, Oladunni Memorial Street, Omiyale Ejigbo, Lagos. Nigeria.

Tel: +2348035395450, +2347010961658
Email: blessed.odira@yahoo.co.uk